About the Author

Sharon King is a writer, advocate, public speaker and above all else, a mum. Through this book she hopes to provide solid, practical advice with regard to being a good friend, sister or mum to that special person in your life who has just received an autism diagnosis for her child.

Of course, this book is dedicated to my wonderful family

Sharon King

HOW BEST TO HELP AN AUTISM MUM

AUSTIN MACAULEY PUBLISHERS™

LONDON • CAMBRIDGE • NEW YORK • SHARJAH

A CIP catalogue record for this title is available from the British Library.

ISBN 9781787105072 (Paperback)
ISBN 9781787105089 (E-Book)
www.austinmacauley.com

First Published (2017)
Austin Macauley Publishers Ltd.
25 Canada Square
Canary Wharf
London
E14 5LQ

Foreword

The idea for this book has been flitting around in my head for about four years now, but, to be fair, I have quite a lot on my plate and the ideal time to sit down and put pen to paper never seemed to present itself. Or if it did, the pen and empty pad had to compete with invitations from my bed, my half-read novel or my television set. Or the telephone rang, or the dog decided that it was time to go for a mid-afternoon walk. Needless to say, the silent call to catalogue my thoughts and experiences as an autism mum has gone unanswered until now.

When I try to think back to those early days during which my children were diagnosed, I can access certain memories. Much of what happened seems to be missing, the bulk of the files have gone astray or been deleted, but fragmented details spring to mind. Images on leaflets, strong coffee in a polystyrene cup, a kind hand placed on my back. These memories, however, come with no emotional connection. I can't remember feeling anything at all. Just a dead absence of feeling that is, in its own way, more frightening than anger or grief.

What a depressing beginning! I hope that this book will be a joyous celebration of the journey that my remarkable children have taken me on, of my metamorphosis from ineffective sleep-walking ghost-mum to the energetic and fulfilled parent that I have become today. I also aim to provide a practical guide as to how best help your friend, sister, or daughter to get the most from her own unique journey. Then why start at such a dark and frightening place, do I hear you ask? Why not start off with a bottle of champers and a few dozen fireworks spelling out the word 'AUTISM' in a beautiful night sky? Here's why; there is every chance that your friend emerged from the clinic following her child's diagnosis feeling that same soulless emptiness, the same disconnected shell-shock that I felt as I sipped the strong coffee from my polystyrene cup and became vaguely aware of the practitioner's kindly hand on my back. The family life that your friend had planned and anticipated has been snatched away from her, before she has even begun to settle into the role of 'Mum'. Be she proud and stoic, open and sharing, distant or close, she has never needed you more than she does now.

Because of my experiences and through this book, I implore you to go on the journey with her, a second in command. I ask you to learn all that you can about the fascinating, complex, elusive condition that is part and parcel of the child that she brought into the world. To quickly dispel a few myths; autism is not a disease. There is no cure and there is no 'growing out of it'. Among those affected by autism are profoundly intellectually disabled people, gifted geniuses and everything in between. Although the recorded prevalence of autism has increased rapidly over the last thirty years, it is not a brand new epidemic. It has always been with us, manifesting in many different ways. I have to force myself to be realistic when I talk about autism, for fear of offending the people who struggle to accept, who struggle to face the very real challenges that this condition presents. But there are many rich and creative gifts that autism brings to us. Autists have an amazing focus of interest, a narrow beam of intense light, their chosen focal point or obsession usurping most (if not all) other endeavours. This autistic focus is the mother of much of our innovation, our inventions. Looking back through history at the lives of great artists, composers, inventors, writers, scientists and engineers, it doesn't take too much imagination to recognise those legendary character traits in the quirky individuals who were unable, or unwilling to follow society's predictable lead. Autism is an integral part of the make-up of many human beings. As our awareness grows, we begin to recognise traits in many more members of society than the (ever increasing) percentage who warrant a diagnosis.

If there were a way to strip autism from a person, then this brutal lobotomy would tear away much of who that person originally was. If there were a way to eradicate autism from our society, then our society would suffer the loss greatly. Healthy society is made up of young and old, male and female, different sexualities and ethnicities. In short, diversity represents Life in all of its splendid assortment. In a society comprised solely of followers, we would be right to ask, who would we look to for leadership? Who would invent, compose and direct? Without these wonderful, original, vulnerable people in our midst, calling out for our care, would we lose incentive, or the ability, to be effective guardians?

Beat Autism! Cure Autism! Against Autism! These are the names of some of 'autism groups' that I have encountered. The names themselves make me shudder. Great change is afoot, there will very soon be a vast shift in our understanding of autism, and in our methods of supporting those with a diagnosis as well as those with obvious traits, but who do not 'tick every box' and have fallen through the diagnosis net. We will know when that change is realised, because our autism groups will then be called 'Support Autism,' 'Embrace Autism' and (I very much hope) 'Love Autism'.

As you begin to know and accept the way that autism affects people, you will realise the importance of making subtle changes your own life, in your home and in your world view. In this way you will find that you are able to accommodate your friend and her newly diagnosed child. Let me promise you, it is not all about sacrifice. It is quite a big ask, I know, but say 'yes' to my invitation, and you will never regret it. Our lives are enriched twenty-fold when we open our hearts and our lives to our autistic brothers and sisters.

Of course there is another bonus. Your friend is going to love you forever.

The Unique Alchemy
of the Family

Conservationists and ornithologists have discovered through trial and error over many decades the importance of respecting the unique alchemy of the nestling family. They don't handle the fertilised eggs, and they don't pick up the chicks, no matter how cute and fluffy, or how strong the desire to attach an identification ring to a brand new pink leg. Outside interference, even if delivered with the most honourable of intentions, can be disastrous. Now, I am not suggesting for one moment that your friend is capable of nudging her newly diagnosed autist from the heights of her family nest. My point is only that too much outside interference at this crucial stage can upset the fine balance of a very delicate situation.

All new mums take time to find their confidence. We have all heard nightmare tales of an interfering mother-in-law or well-meaning friend barging in, taking over, whipping the blanket of self-reliance from beneath the new mum's feet. At the time of her child's diagnosis, the little one is generally well past the 'new baby' stage. Mum's confidence will almost definitely 'go back to Old Kent Road', not passing 'Go', or collecting £200.

Whether she has received this diagnosis, or questions have been raised and it is still in the pipeline, Mum is sure to be reviewing the effectiveness of her parenting skills right now. There is a dark history of blame attached to the causes of autism. Over the past few decades there have been a handful of pioneering professionals who have misguidedly looked towards the mother's behaviour in their search for the cause of autism. Someone must be to blame here! When it comes to children and their behaviour (especially when that behaviour is deemed to be 'bad' or 'outside the norm') it is, of course, one of our great traditions to blame the parents. In the not so distant past, children have been removed from the care of their parents, based on the fallout from this dangerous and misguided presumption. Thankfully we live in more enlightened times and progress in our understanding of autism is moving forward all the time. But still, the echoes of this heart breaking 'blame the cold mother' notion still haunt us today.

Whether she is aware of this tragic history or not, your friend is now in a position where she must open the doors of her home to all kinds of people. Speech therapists, occupational therapists, social workers and play specialists; this list can seem endless. Depending largely on the size of the ego of the visiting professionals, this can be a blessing or a curse. I still remember Joyce and Barbara, my ladies from the Portage early development service, who visited us on Friday mornings before Daisy and Lenny started pre-school nursery. The Portage service was excellent, an absolute god-send. These ladies would bring different goodies each week from the local toy library. They were highly skilled in play observation and were able to explain to me the many vital stages in the development of play. With typically developing children this process happens so fast it is almost unobservable, like the many different slides of a stop-motion animation, you would need to slow the movie down considerably in order to fully appreciate the nature of each one of the slides. This development of play seems fluid, seamless. When observing our typically developing children it is almost impossible to keep up. We notice the acquisition of one skill, we turn our heads for a moment, and this skill has developed in five different ways. It's a domino effect branching outwards as well as moving along. The child acquires many new skills within a dizzying short space of time. It is breathtaking and beautiful.

Play for the child with autism develops very differently, but to watch on and be involved in the acquisition of these new play skills can be just as exquisite. In many ways I am happy for this slowed down version of my younger two children's toppling dominos. It is an absolute pleasure to be able to track and fully appreciate the wonder of these many stages of development. I didn't always feel so positive about my children's slow or off kilter development, of course. In those early days when my friends' children were learning to speak, to play, to ask questions about the world that they were part of, I wanted nothing more than to speed my children up a bit, to push or to lure them into a shape of normality.

Joyce (and then Barbara who came after her) was at my side each Friday morning, as I patiently presented inset trays, skittles, mirrored carousels and other enticing toys. These ladies were there to support my demonstration of the toys when I became dispirited. They would take over for half an hour while I sipped tea and watched on, once removed, but still very much involved. Joyce and Barbara were also there to answer my many questions.

I was fully in the dark back then. I wasn't even sure that that all children with learning disabilities went to school. I didn't have the courage to voice this particular concern, but I wasn't even sure that all disabled children were allowed to live at home. I had a vague notion of doctors turning up at my door in the middle of the night, packing the children off in a van. It seems crazy to admit that now, but my early parenting experience was infused with constant fear, a mistrust of the outer world. Much of the way that I felt, I realise now, was a direct result of the brutally insensitive way that I was initially informed of Daisy's disability. If this situation had been managed more considerately, and I had been provided with suitable information and support in those early days, I believe that I would have been saved years of bewilderment and negativity. More to the point, my children would have gotten off to a much better start in life.

Not only was I in the dark about my rights, and my children's rights, about what kind of shape our family life was likely to take, I felt that even if I were ever to find the courage to admit that I didn't know any of this stuff, I would have had no idea where to take my questions. In our Friday play sessions, my friendships with Joyce and Barbara developed naturally, and our conversations gradually addressed the awkward issues that were on my mind. Plus, I had someone to have a cup of coffee and a donut with, which I find helps in any situation.

Both Joyce and Barbara were lovely, kind, gentle and knowledgeable, without claiming to be experts in every aspect of every possible condition. If they didn't have the answer to a particular question, they could direct me to someone who was more likely to be able to help.

Nice, kind, gentle professionals, who did not profess to know everything. Ah, if only there were more of these to go around! Not every professional is so well balanced, so respectful of the delicate balance of Mum's mental wellbeing, of her wavering confidence and of how this can affect the whole of the family dynamic.

The mum with a newly diagnosed child is going through the agonising process of absorbing and assimilating this new and life-changing information about her little one. At the same time, she is also very much aware that she is under intense scrutiny. Your friend may feel that her home, formerly a cosy, private, sanctuary, has been blasted away. Instead she is now forced to live in a glass house, with a tour bus load of specialists peering in, moving through, making notes, judging. How is she faring? What conclusions are these professionals drawing about her? Their judgements will be closely linked to the rate of her child's development, or to the natural path of that development, she feels. Based on observable evidence, she sees only that she is failing.

And on top of the professional scrutiny and advice, other words of wisdom will be flying in her direction. Shell-shocked from her child's impending or actual diagnosis, the advice being fired at her from every angle feels like deadly bullets in a war zone. Who should she listen to? Missiles of opposite information can be fired at the same time from different weapons. Well meaning (but completely misguided) friends may be adamant that she should ignore this cruel diagnosis, or the threat of it, they add to the confusion by assuring her that her child is completely normal. Maybe just taking a little extra time to reach his milestones, but what the hey? They all get there in the end, don't they? She should treat him 'normally' and wait for him to develop. Normally.

Mum's critics may be telling her that she has overindulged her baby or her toddler. That she hasn't metered out the discipline, she hasn't invested her energy into organising a proper bedtime routine, and this is why her child isn't sleeping. Need she pick him up every time he cries, for heavens' sake? Must she pander to her toddler's weird fear of different foods being mixed together? To his princely insistence that she buys certain brands, or that his sandwiches be presented in triangles, but never, ever, squares? Should she really allow him to watch the same episode of *Thomas the Tank Engine* over and over again? No wonder her child is acting strangely, with all of these weird behaviours being reinforced and encouraged! (Heavy sarcasm here, for any of you literal thinkers.)

Maybe your autism mum has a friend with some limited experience of autism, who is offering up her account as the only possible path that this story will follow. I hope, for your friend's sake, that she doesn't have one of these, because they're bloody unbearable. 'They accused my nephew Christopher of having autism when he was a little boy. He didn't speak in sentences until he was six, and now he has a PhD in nuclear physics. Clearly there was never anything wrong with him after all! Get him on a gluten free diet, teach him how to use a computer, and the problem will sort itself out.'

There may be another 'friend' whispering in Mum's ear that she suspected that this diagnosis was in the pipeline all along. We all have a love of being right, of second guessing the outcomes of life like a real-time version of 'who-done-it?' – but really, what pleasure can there ever be in raking self-righteous 'I told you so' points from a difficult and painful situation such as this?

The wise friend will instinctively know that she should step back at this time, offering company and comfort, but sitting on her advice until she is sure that it is valid and required. Being a receptacle for outpourings is the kindest stance to take. However strong the temptation to tell her that everything will be OK, please resist. In all honesty, you don't know if things will be OK or not. The odds are, if your friend has been guided towards having her child assessed for autism, the process will result in a positive diagnosis. When a child has a diagnosis of autism, there will be a lot of hard work involved for the parent, and the child's life will take an entirely different course to the one that he would have otherwise had. Given the right support, though, things can work out well for your friend and her family in the long term. Now, though, is a time of grief. Your friend will and should mourn the version of family life that she had felt was her birth-right. Her mourning period could go on for some time. Once this period is over, there will be many joyful times to share with your friend and her child, but for now, be a source of comfort as she processes this new information. Respect the unique relationship that is developing between your Mother-bird and her unusual hatchling. She may not do things the way that would. For many reasons, she may not be able to. But that is OK. As her trusted second in command, you are never over-bearing or dictatorial, because you understand how much she is going to need her confidence in the future. Her confidence has taken a knock, but reassure your friend that it is still there, a punch drunk boxer with tweeting birds circling its head, stunned, but waiting for the recovery that will come with time.

Your job for now is simply to be there and to respect the magical alchemy within your friend's particular nest.

Diagnosis Days

The first of my children to be diagnosed was my middle daughter, Daisy. Her diagnosis was not autism, however, but a rare genetic disorder called Kabuki Syndrome. The pregnancy had been largely non-eventful, although I do remember being concerned at times that she didn't move around in-utero so much as her restless, kick-boxing older sister. The birth was traumatic, a twenty-two-hour labour during which I enthusiastically sucked the life out of three full canisters of gas and air. Light headed with pain and drugs, I would have agreed to anything.

The traumatic process was intercepted at the final moment due to baby's bottom presenting instead of her head. Despite a thorough early-labour examination, in which the midwife proudly boasted being able to feel baby's head, arms and legs, and reassuring me that everything was in the perfect position for a smooth and easy delivery, my baby was firmly settled in the notoriously difficult breach position. She was stuck and would need considerable assistance to get safely into the wider world. Due to her distress, she had released her first sludgy-green poo before being dragged out of my womb. This was very dangerous, I was told, poisonous and potentially life-threatening for her and likely to cause gruesome complications for me. An emergency C-section was quickly arranged, and my new daughter was eased out, sponged down, and delivered quietly into my arms. Drugged to the nines, I was quite calm and philosophical about the whole affair.

But my baby didn't cry. Instead, she peered owl-like at her new and clinical environment. Instantly, I fell in love. She was adorable, her face and shoulders being covered in down-like peach fuzz. Her blue eyes were almond shaped and her mouth tiny. Surprisingly, she didn't share her older sister's delicate, elfin features. Her nose was snub, her face full. I had planned to call her Ruby, but she didn't look the way I had expected her to look at all. I had foolishly supposed that she would be an identikit version of her older sister. Throughout my pregnancy I had been sure that she was a girl, and in my romantic mind's eye I had pictured the two sisters walking hand in hand, almost indistinguishable in matching pig-tails and floral dresses. Despite this baby's unfamiliar features and colouring, I felt a pull of recognition, as though I had known her for all of my life. The change of identity called for a change of name, and Ruby quickly became Daisy.

Despite her worryingly small head circumference, her silence made her wise in my eyes. Golden tufts hinted at the halo of curls that would follow. She latched onto the breast like a pro, and we were left to our bonding business.

Throughout the next few days, however, various professionals came to peer and to poke. I just wanted them to go away, to leave us to whatever fate had in store for us. I was fiercely protective of my beautiful new daughter. I felt energy within the room above and beyond the cocoon of new motherhood that surrounded me. It was all a bit suspicious, and as the morphine haze dissipated, post narcotic paranoia set in, and I became convinced that there was something going on.

My husband Richard was on paternity leave from work, visiting each day, but spending the majority of his time caring for and entertaining our toddler, Rosie. At twenty months Rosie was charming, alert, and a bit of a handful. I very much looked forward to their visits, to the take-away food and news from the real world that they brought with them. I loved it when Rosie climbed on the hospital bed to cuddle up with me. We read stories together and talked about all of the things that we would do once Daisy and I were allowed to come home. Looking back now, I see that Rosie was little more than a baby herself, but even then we treated one another as equals. We were best friends, and we longed for normality to resume, so that we could be back together again.

On the third day after Daisy's birth I was getting very ratty (There is a medically proven fact about that third day, a dip in something that causes a temporary depression. I could Google it for research purposes, but I am sure you are at least as familiar with search engines as I am, so I will leave it to you, should you feel motivated.). I really did not appreciate being detained in hospital, a criminal unsure of the nature of the crime that I had committed. Each time a member of the nursing team paid me a visit, I informed them that I would be leaving very shortly. Frustratingly, none of the nurses seemed convinced.

I remember that third evening, desperately attempting to force my tired eyes and brain to process the words of a novel that I had been reading enthusiastically before

Daisy's birth. My new daughter was sleeping soundly, but still, I was failing miserably at the task in hand. The presence of a Junior Registrar hovering over Daisy's transparent hospital cot, his furrowed brow far easier to read than the words of my novel, was not exactly helping.

'Is there something wrong?' I snapped, eventually.

'This baby isn't normal. She has some kind of syndrome,' the helpful professional informed me (Yes, more heavy sarcasm here. You'll get used to it. If you know me, you'll already be used to it.).

'Down's Syndrome?' I heard my voice ask of the registrar.

'Yes. Or something similar. The muscle tone seems low and the feet are too small, see?'

I couldn't really see anything but a beautiful baby, but I nodded anyway.

The Registrar left then. It felt like I had been brutally dropped into a deep, dark hole. It was lonely down there. A thousand questions bubbled inside me, begging to be answered, but there was nobody to supply the answers that I needed. I scooped Daisy up from the plastic bedside cot, seated her on the bridge of my knelt-up thighs, and examined my sleeping daughter. She was the only person who could answer my unspoken questions, but her almond eyes were resolutely closed and her tiny lips were sealed. I knew, though, that whatever the future held, Daisy and I were in it together. Sad as I was, nothing on earth could compare with the overwhelming feeling of love and protection that surged through me. We sat like this for hours, Daisy and I, until she woke for another gentle feed. Afterwards, I settled her back in the cot, covered her with

Grandma's hand-crocheted blanket, and phoned Richard to keep him up to speed with the vague yet savage conclusion that the Registrar had drawn.

'They're saying that there's something wrong with the baby,' I told him. I couldn't really think of a kinder way to put it. I still remember the sound of my own words, treacherously adding weight to the registrar's cruel conclusion.

Of course, my husband was angry. How could a professional even consider firing such life altering news at a newly delivered mother, while she had nobody to support her in absorbing and processing the information? It was to be another fourteen months, in a different hospital room, with a far more experienced professional, when we would receive Daisy's formal diagnosis. The geneticist at St James' in Leeds would tell us that Daisy's condition, Kabuki Syndrome, was rare, that there wasn't that much information available, but that I should think carefully before planning another pregnancy, as a genetic link was not out of the question. By that time, though, I was six months pregnant with Lenny (part of me wonders now how the geneticist could have failed to notice this fact, but I guess people come in all shapes and sizes and who was he to take a guess at the shape that a pre-pregnant me might take?).

Cut to September 2004. (Please excuse the chronological hopscotch, but it's a difficult story to pin down, time-wise). Rosie was five years old, and growing up fast. Not in the typical way that my friend's children were maturing, though. She was a sponge for information. She could converse very easily, as she had learned to speak in sentences at around eighteen months of age. She loved nothing more than to chat with adults; it often seemed that conversations with her peers were a little beneath her. Rosie was full of questions, about everything imaginable. Her questions didn't always centre on the physical plane either. Like her mother, she was very philosophical, and asked questions about the past, about the human soul, about the nature of reality. We did everything together, twin spirits, the best of friends.

We had some great discussions, Rosie and I. One time, while she was drawing with crayons in the dining room, she turned her sweet little pixie-face to me and said, 'Remember that dream I had last night, Mummy?'

Used to her offbeat conversational style as I was, this line of questioning took me by surprise. 'How can I remember your dream? I have my dreams, and you have yours. If you tell me your dream, I'll know about it. You haven't told me your dream yet...' Rosie looked at me with intense suspicion, like I was a deceiver, a crazy woman. Evidently, it had never entered her head that I wasn't privy to her every thought, her every imagining. This 'presumed shared knowledge' is one of the key testing points for autism, I was later to discover. Back then it was just another little puzzle in the precocious, random development of my eldest daughter.

I couldn't allow myself to get too worried about these little idiosyncrasies. Rosie was so bright. She was a peculiar genius. A prodigy, I was sure. And anyway, I had so much else going on that I really didn't have the time to ponder these trivial mysteries.

Daisy, at four years old was significantly behind in her development. She was only just sitting up and not yet making any indication that she understood language. She didn't babble; her cries were the open-mouthed vowel-sounds of a very young baby. I could easily distinguish between a happy noise and a sad one, but that seemed to be the beginning and end of the range of her verbal communication. I still held her lidded beaker and supported her head as she drank. I spooned nutritious mush into her tiny mouth with a doll's spoon, always vigilant against choking.

After much deliberation and persuasion on our part, we had convinced the local primary school that a two day a week inclusion placement was the best option for Daisy. This way, Daisy got to make friends in the community, I had the opportunity to take her to nursery on a Monday and Tuesday, but for the remainder of the week, she boarded the school bus and was escorted to an excellent special school on the other side of town. The arrangement was the compromising result of much inter-marital quarrelling and an energy-consuming campaign for changes to the local education authority's school placement rules, but more of this later.

It transpired that Daisy's condition affected the development of her immunity as well as her physical body and her learning. Time and time again, Daisy picked up every nasty from tonsillitis, to pneumonia and meningitis. There were a host of other malevolent bugs that brewed, none specific and nameless, reddening her chubby cheeks and spoiling her appetite.

With Daisy's bag always packed for the hospital, we were relieved that our toddler, Lenny, was such a healthy little chap. He had literally never been ill. His appetite was ferocious and his muscle tone glorious. At eight months he stood in his cot, abs clearly defined beneath his preferred nightwear of a disposable nappy. He would drink cockily from his milk bottle with one hand on his hip, in the manner that a seventeen-year-old might drink a bottle of beer. He didn't need to be winded. He would let out a manly belch and then throw the bottle across the room, to alert us to the fact that it was empty, and he wanted to get out of the cot. A few weeks down the line he was easily able to scale the white wooden bars of his own accord, so we opted let the cot side down, arranging pillows to break a midnight fall that never came. He settled quickly into our bed, forgetting that he had one of his own. I was repeatedly offered the advice that babies shouldn't sleep with their parents, for the danger of being crushed. Looking at his muscle tone and the bulk of him, we joked that we were the ones in danger. Lenny settled into a routine of non-routine, doing his own thing, ruling roost.

The months went by, and still our son didn't speak. It was another mystery. He liked certain books, ones with real-life pictures instead of illustrations. He needed little encouragement to open these books but stubbornly refused to share. He much preferred to take his beloved books to a quiet place, under the dining table or behind the sofa, where he would focus intently on his preferred images (usually of biscuits or cakes). He would stare and stare at the photographs on the board books. Sometimes, he would take a crayon and scribble over these beloved pictures, then stare even closer, trying to locate the biscuit hidden beneath the scribbles. There were multi-coloured scribbles all over the walls and furniture. We took to hiding the felt-tips and the crayons and Rosie composed a little song committing the situation to legend – 'Lens, Lens, banned from pens.'

I needed my son to speak. Rosie was normal (please God, Rosie was normal), and OK, Daisy had this rare condition, but as soon as Lenny began speaking, as soon as he could prove his normalcy in this way, then I could relax. I would be vindicated. Despite my overwhelming love for Daisy, I felt that one unusual child in the family was quite enough.

Many of my waking hours were spent trying to convince Lenny to step into this normal mould. To speak. To point. To enjoy a game of 'round and round the garden,' for Christ's sake! But no, stubbornly, my man-boy continued to develop in his own particular, peculiar and inimitable way. I simply couldn't agree with people who suggested that Lenny had some kind of developmental delay. As a result of my experience with Daisy, I knew developmental delay like the back of my hand, and this boy wasn't delayed. He was, without doubt, progressing. His progression was taking a different path, a bizarre irregular path, but, even accounting for this, I was adamant that in his own roundabout way, he was generally moving forwards.

At last, a breakthrough on a caravan holiday! I remember a lovely evening after a day at the beach, a fish and chip supper, with six-year-old Rosie sitting at the Formica table, drawing. Daisy, enjoying a rare window of good health, was snuggled happily on my knee. We were singing together, Rosie, Richard and I, trying our best to attract Lenny's attention. We tempted him with pop songs, television show theme-tunes, nursery rhymes. We tried an old family favourite, The Owl and the Pussycat. No luck. At the penultimate stage of 'Twinkle Twinkle Little Star,' we all stopped in unison, turning to Lenny who danced up and down the caravan with a piece of Brio in each hand. He stopped his endless back and forth running and looked back at me, giving full and direct eye contact. 'Are!' he said, completing the song.

How we all laughed! How happy I was. He got it, he could speak! We thoroughly enjoyed the rest of that holiday, buoyant and joyful, invigorated with the certainty that our boy was completely normal, and that because he was normal, our little family was saved.

But we were wrong. As the weeks turned into months, that solitary 'are' at the end of 'Twinkle Twinkle' was not repeated, or joined by any new words. My son's gruff little voice made all kinds of noises, but none of them were discernable. It seemed that his noises were unintentional, like respiration, or digestion, they happened all on their own. Lenny still did not point. His eye contact was atypical, either missing altogether or fierce and penetrating. Apparently, he saw no value in toilet training but took against wearing a nappy. My days were spent following him around, trying to intercept every perfect arc of wee.

Lenny held on to cherished objects, but they were hardly the type of things that seemed worthy of adoration. A headless Barbie, limbs secured in place with black tape. A plastic coat-hanger. A Peter Kay DVD cover ('Oh, does he like Peter Kay?' a confused friend asked, on noticing the DVD cover tucked firmly underneath my toddler's arm. 'No,' I replied. 'He's doesn't know who Peter Kay is.')

Lenny was diagnosed with classic autism just before his third birthday. I instinctively knew the truth of it, but at the same time it didn't seem real. Whereas I had been quite excited to tell people about Daisy's diagnosis eighteen months earlier, (at last an answer! At last a word to fend off the constant barrage of questions, to describe my little daughter's peculiarities) this new autism diagnosis seemed a step too far. My younger two children had been diagnosed with life-long learning conditions in such a short space of time. I struggled to tell people, even the people who had been following Lenny's progress with sincere, well-meaning interest. I even struggled to tell the people who were my friends. The word 'autism' stuck somewhere in my throat. It seemed hurtful, painful and cruel.

But as the months went by and we learned more about it, we became more used to the diagnosis. Directly or indirectly our family and friends found out. They didn't seem to blame us. Life went on as normal (though our version of normal was quite different from other people's). The three-page leaflet that was given to us as a point of reference for Daisy's rare genetic condition was swamped beneath the many books about autism that I quickly amassed. I bought some, and others were donated to my worthy cause. An avid reader, I gobbled up everything available. Autism was such an interesting condition! And, as well as being utterly exhausting to parent, Lenny was also a very interesting little boy, a real character.

We met other classically autistic children and couldn't fail to notice the behavioural similarities between them and our son. And we gradually got to know other, more able young people, who were also affected by autism but in vastly different ways. They were able to speak and they could follow instructions. It struck me that these children seemed to engage in all-consuming hobbies, and I quickly learned that to tap in to these obsessions was a conversational hit. Developmentally, these kids seemed a million miles away from my son, but I recognised some of the same underlying issues.

Rosie absorbed the news about her brother's diagnosis with typical wisdom. 'He'll always be Len-Lens,' she said, solemnly.

I bought her a book, *Little Rainman – Autism through the eyes of a child*. I was sure that it would help her to understand. It's a short book of only 68 pages, nicely illustrated, and describes the life of a non-verbal boy called Jonathan. From Jonathan's viewpoint, the reader is shown how he hates certain colours, how he has difficulties with balance. How he loves to spin and to dance. Seven-year-old Rosie read the book in one sitting, her beautiful hazel eyes focused intently on the words. She didn't break off once in the hour and a half it took her to absorb the story. Once the book was finished she closed it, placed it carefully back on the bookshelf and came to sit next to me. She took my hand and looked deeply into my eyes.

She said, 'Mum, I have autism too.'

Getting Out

The first thing that occurs to me when I consider the problem, 'how best to help an autism mum?' is that it is vital for your friend to continue to get out and about with her child, in order that they can establish themselves as part of their community. Like it or not, we are a societal animal. Even for the most self-sufficient, or the shyest amongst us, this is an inescapable truth.

For the sake of her mental health, and of the varied and stimulating environment that is supportive to any child's development, your friend needs to take that giant leap into the big wide world.

Before we start to think of ways to support this essential integration, though, it is useful to think carefully about the kind of things that may be holding her back, and the very real reasons that she may have for retreating to her lair.

A point I laboured earlier; your friend's confidence has taken a giant kicking. A sudden confidence setback is reason enough for anyone to hole themselves up in the comfortable prison of their home, to start making online grocery orders and to decline intrusive invitations. Your friend could well be worried about hostile reactions to her child. The weight of the diagnosis will be heavy on her, almost pinning her to the spot. She knows that when she does go out, there will be inevitable questions. Just as all roads lead to Rome, even the most innocent or light hearted of conversations will eventually end up in the same place, and she will be forced to say that word aloud.

'Autism.'

'He has autism.'

'That's because of his autism.'

'He's autistic. He was diagnosed last week.'

I practiced a few times in the mirror before taking newly diagnosed Lenny to a church led toddler's group. 'He has autism!' I tested the words out, enthusiastically, with a smile. No, that seemed a tad too manic, didn't quite fit the remit. 'He's autistic,' with an air of sadness, a sage nod of the head. Too depressing, not quite the way I truly felt about my vibrant, robust little boy. 'Well…you know how he refuses to share? How he always plays with the same plastic light-up teddy bear? How he uses my finger as a tool to push the buttons instead of using his own? Well, that's all because he's autistic! Ta-da!'

Because the concept of autism was so unfamiliar to me, still resting on the surface of my understanding, not quite 'bedded in' yet, it was very difficult for me to even imagine passing the information on in a natural way. Even if I were to perfect the words, I knew that my expression and countenance would betray me. My vulnerability would be there on my face for all the world to see. This went against everything that I knew about myself. I wanted to be strong and certain, not weak and dithery.

Looking back, revisiting my tentative initial judgements around the subject of autism, I can hardly relate to those feelings at all. When I speak about my children now (I do, all of the time, and I'm sure people get sick of hearing about my precious brood), I am animated, excited, bursting with pride. Today, when I say the word 'autism,' I speak of individuality, creativity, unique thinking and beautiful, candid honesty. Rosie, Daisy and Lenny have painted my life, tying a colourful rainbow around my understanding of the world.

Back then, though, the word 'autism' carried images of disturbed, unreachable and unlovable children rocking violently in empty rooms. Expressionless and remote, the word was grey and cold, and evoked a hollow, empty feeling. Experience and circumstance has certainly pushed my understanding a long way over the last ten years.

But enough about my journey for now; back to your friend and her little one. At this absolutely crucial point in her child's development, a stage where he desperately needs to begin to push the boundaries of his experience and taste the treasures of the wider world, Mum is feeling decidedly shaky. Let's say she does retreat to her lair. Let's put ourselves in her shoes and imagine that she is more than happy to settle back into the cosy toddler's world that she and her child have inhabited for the past few years. A pre-schooler's world is cossetted and comfortable. A world of quiet afternoon naps, nursery rhymes and treasured toys. A world of buttered toast fingers and cheerfully illustrated storybooks. A predictable, warm and protected universe. Given the circumstances, who can blame the fledgling autist, with his enhanced love of familiarity and his natural resistance to change, if he settles back nicely into this familiar habitat? It's the easy option, but your friend could be setting up major trouble for herself in the years to come. Those legendary 'terrible twos' can take on an alarming new dimension when coupled with a diagnosis of autism.

While routine is supportive and reassuring for children with autism, it can be a double-edged sword. I have met many mums who have become absolute slaves to their child's rigid schedule. Completely controlled by her little one's wants and desires, Mum's old life fades away, the practicalities of working around his complex agenda leaving no space at all for the things that she used to hold dear.

Weaving regular outings and trips into the pre-school autist's routine is excellent practice. It may seem much easier to take a midnight trip to the supermarket leaving the little one to his dad's slumbering care, or to politely decline playdates and lunch invitations. Sticking to what is safe and manageable rather than risk that fabled meltdown can become a dangerous habit. The thing with invites and turning them down is this, three or four excuses down the line and the invites generally dry up. It can become a downwards, isolating spiral for both mother and child.

It is far better in the long run for your friend to brace herself, accept the fact that interaction with the outside world brings both challenge and joy, and to purposefully begin to widen the day to day experience of her toddler. Here's how you can help.

Firstly, you are providing an invaluable service simply by being with her, by giving that nudge, if it is necessary. It is infinitely more tempting to stay at home if there are no invitations to bat away.

Once she is out, having a non-judgemental ally by her side, someone with whom to laugh off a failure or an aborted mission, makes any situation more bearable. Imagine tripping up in a public place, when you are alone. The painful awkwardness, the nervous sound of your own laughter. The embarrassment that follows is usually far more excruciating than the mishap that caused it. What a different situation entirely if you are with a friend, the trip becomes a joke, easily laughed off, the slight humiliation shared, halved, gone in moments.

To help to entice her, you can research and plan days out for the three of you. One of the key elements of depression is a lack of motivation, and a lack of impetus to plan ahead. Your friend may well be suffering from depression as a result of the sudden changes in her life. If she is sleep deprived as well as being depressed, then Mum is likely to be 'treading water,' merely staying afloat, keeping on top of her day to day tasks and appointments, with little enthusiasm left for looking ahead, or planning something fun. Of course, you must be very sensitive not to be too pushy. You could gently suggest an afternoon together, and once she has agreed, ask her to leave it to you to book something exciting, your treat, all she needs to do is to be ready on time!

A trip to the zoo, local play farm or funfair may seem ambitious at this stage of the game, and, of course, you will be mindful not to plan anything that could result in an alarming reaction from your friend's child. This could be disastrous, and trigger your friend's further retreat from society. Instead, go for something laid back and safe, like a nature walk, a quiet lunch in a café, or a picnic by a river. As your relationship with the child grows, you will become more familiar with what kind of activities work best, but until then, err on the side of caution, and think gentle and relaxing.

Another great service you can do your friend is to be on hand to offer her child a distraction, in the event of a meltdown.

Meltdowns can be very distressing for all concerned, and tend to occur because of overstimulation. The casual observer will see a spoiled child trying to get his own way. Those of us in the know realise that people with autism are far less able to filter out information than neurotypicals are. The best insight into overstimulation that I have heard to date goes a little bit like this. Imagine wearing a shirt made of sandpaper. At the same time, you are wearing earphones pumping loud rock music directly into your auditory canals. Also, there is a wedge of acidic lemon in your mouth. Stuffed into your nostrils are two wads of cotton wool, soaked with bleach. As though this wasn't enough, someone is shining twin torches into your eyes. Despite all of this cruel and painful stimulation, you are still being bombarded with instructions, you are being asked to complete tasks, to converse with people that you don't know. How many of us could compliantly plod on in these circumstances, without exhibiting some kind of breakdown reaction?

Once we understand the causes of meltdown, it is easy to see that a child going through this reaction to intense stimulus needs help and not punishment. He needs space, and peace. The last thing he needs in the world is to be the focus of a gathering crowd of onlookers, shaking their heads, pointing, laughing or tutting away in their mistaken assumption that a basic lack of parenting lies behind this brattish display.

You can be of great assistance when it comes to the distributing of advice to the gathering crowd of interested on-lookers. This is not free entertainment, nor is it an opportunity for the smug general populous at the shopping centre to utter predictable phrases that always seem to begin with the tired old words 'In my day…' or 'If that kid was mine…'

I always say that if people have the time to stand and stare, then they have the time to offer assistance. Often, outsiders simply cannot help in this scenario, extra bodies, extra words, extra interference only means more stimulus for the child and add to the pain of the situation.

Scatter this thoughtless crowd with your assertiveness, and your friend will then be able to concentrate all of her best efforts on returning her child to a state of calm, or at least removing him from the intense environment that triggered the temporary breakdown.

'While your fascination with this spectacle is completely understandable, we ask that you kindly step away from the screaming child and give everyone a bit of space…' (or words to that effect, perhaps you know some more direct phrases that will more speedily disperse the crowd?)

As you get to know the little autist in your life, it will become clear to you exactly what treats and motivators will prove the most useful, should a tricky situation crop up.

Daisy has always held a fascination for bright fabrics, the more bizarrely patterned the better. This seemingly innocuous passion has been at the root of some extremely awkward situations in the past. I remember a dinner in a cheap and cheerful '2 for 1' family restaurant. Daisy had to be bodily removed from a fellow diner, who's pink and white spotty dress proved to be just too tempting. Sticky fingered and determined, she lost sight of any other goal;

she wanted only to pat this heavenly material. Even after she had been safely secured back into her wheelchair, and rolled back to our table, she continued to reach out, desperate to touch this mesmerising fabric, crying mournfully, banging her head against the table in sheer frustration. Her gammon and pineapple remained untouched, the teatime ambiance was shattered, and the lady in pin polka dots finished off her meal and left, looking fashionably uncomfortable.

There is always a remedy! Rather than be beaten down by the many little hurdles that life presents, I try to see each problem as a work-out for my versatility. Among other goodies, we now carry a tin of sparkly fabric off-cuts when we go out. These scraps of material provide a handy diversion should Daisy's attention be commandeered by a brightly dressed stranger.

A little thought and consideration and twenty minutes of your time can produce a similarly tempting goody bag at very little cost to yourself. Favourite sweets, a tub of bubbles, spinning tops or squares of pretty fabric. Needless to say, different motivators work for different children. I have a friend whose fourteen-year-old autist is obsessed with shiny objects. She always carries foil-wrapped Oxo cubes in her bag, as handling them seems to relax her son in any situation. If ever an emergency jug of gravy is required, then she will be my girl! I wear chunky bangles, I have a whole box of them, usually purchased from the charity shop for pennies. In an emergency situation they can be removed from my wrist, and used as spinners, entertaining Daisy and Lenny for the twenty minutes or so that it might take between ordering and being served with a meal in a restaurant. Coins can also be very useful, you usually have a few about your person, and a few sessions down the line, you too could become an expert spinner! Being prepared is the key to successful outings, and these low-cost treasures can be held back; reserved for difficult moments, to delight and to motivate, to reinforce your relationship with your friend's child, and to make simple outings doable.

Let me assure you, the background security that comes with knowing that your magician's sleeves are stuffed with these practical tricks and surprises will increase your confidence. You are tooled up, you are armed! Your mission will succeed. Like most children, little autists are experts at picking up on these subliminal messages. They tend to 'just know' when we are confident, when we mean business. Your confidence helps them to sense their behavioural boundaries, and makes them feel safe. All children are hardwired to push against these boundaries, while secretly craving the reassurance that their own good behaviour is what is expected, and is achievable.

Parties, the attending of which is probably the greatest pleasure for the majority of the population, often cause much stress and anxiety for the family coping with autism. I always find it ironic that the things that are the highlight of most people's lives can be a bit of a nightmare for us. Of course, if we are invited, we very much want to attend. We want to put our best foot forward, our glad rags on, and join in the celebrations.

However, with the best will in the world, things can, and frequently do, go wrong.

When it comes to parties, we've had a few disasters over the years. I can close my eyes now and snapshots of these calamities are replayed like a spliced-together disaster movie. I see quick fingers grabbing the elaborate icing from a beautiful wedding cake, the sweet bounty being crammed into my son's eager mouth before speed and agility allowed me to even get off my seat. I see Lenny blowing out the Easter Candle in a Catholic church celebration (a christening, I think). I laughed off this monkey-business at the time, but later learned that this candle should remain eternally lit, and should it chance to be snuffed, then the consequences for humanity are darkly serious. Nice afternoon's work, Len. Lenny again, I see a speedy disrobing (how my boy loved to be naked, when he was younger) before a Benny Hill style chase around a community centre (in fairness, my friend's husband had neglected to book a strip-a-gram for her fiftieth birthday…).

These days, we tend to receive invitations with cautious optimism. We often opt to hire a sitter, if there is anyone with the skills, patience and inclination available. Some invitations come with the advice 'no children, thank you' – the sitter is hired, or the respite placement dutifully booked, only for us to discover on the evening of the event that other people's children have managed to escape these age-based sanctions, or have slipped through the net. Whilst under certain circumstances this is understandable, I'd be lying if I were to say that it doesn't hurt.

When we received an invitation for the wedding of our nephew a couple of years ago, it was clear that Daisy and Lenny were definitely on the guest list. We dressed in our Sunday finest, packed our bag of essentials with tried and tested motivators and treats, gritted our teeth and hoped for the best.

Words can't express how touched and grateful we were when, on entering the venue, we discovered that our nephew's new bride had sourced, purchased and presented an array of sensory toys to help keep Daisy and Lenny entertained throughout the proceedings. The tiny bubbles that we blew from the beautiful miniature bottles hardly seemed out of place at the wedding reception. Luminous balls pinged between tables and our little darlings provided the agreeable background noise of contented humming and played happily all afternoon.

Best of all, though, this thoughtful gesture gave us a very clear message. *Our unusual little family was wanted.* On this occasion we, and our children, were very welcome.

My ambition for your friend is that she never need question the sincerity of any invitation that she receives. I see it as a problem that needs to be tackled from all angles. On her part, her confidence will be greater if she is well prepared. Supported by you, she can be self-assured and optimistic. She can do her very best to teach her child the fundamental rules of sociably acceptable behaviour, and even in the cases of the most challenging of children, with determination, great progress can quickly be made in this area.

But with the best will in the world, if the societal understanding is not there, if every wrong move is punished by disapproving stares or the soul-destroying echoes of 'tut-tut,' then she will begin to lose the will to be involved at all. And so lies the road to loneliness.

Supporting Friendships

We, mums, worry about our children's friendships – it's what we do! Regardless of the fact that our autistic children may not particularly desire traditional friendships and may even find forced social situations deeply uncomfortable, we continue to insist. Eyes firmly on the prize of social acceptance for our children, we plough on, inviting potential buddies for tea, cheerily insisting that the various disinterested parties engage in turn-taking games, sending home cake and goody bags with the half-hearted hopeful parting words 'come back soon!'

Although Lenny is largely clueless when it comes to forging and maintaining friendships, he does love being around people. We have a lively household with frequent visitors and he genuinely seems to enjoy being part of the throng. When we go out to our favourite parks and playgrounds, he doesn't actively engage people, unless he has managed to procure a chocolate biscuit and cannot work out how to remove the wrapper – and even under these desperate circumstances he will approach an adult, and not risk handing over his precious booty to another child. Lenny, though, is delighted by the antics of other children, especially if they are running around him, showing off their skate-board stunts or playing football. Although he may lack the know-how or the incentive to join in, there is no doubt at all that he is able to pick up on the euphoric mood.

Rosie has always been very picky when it comes to friends. She loves to spend time around people with the same interests as her, and her peer group currently comprises a handful of loyal girlfriends who she has known since primary school, and an eclectic assortment of autistic teenage boys who share her love of superheroes. Her militant stance when it comes to any suggestion of bigotry, chauvinism or misogyny constantly jeopardises her friendships with these Marvel and DC obsessed boys, and I have often felt pushed into the role of peacemaker, wearily doling out advice, and attempting to sooth the constantly erupting volcano of her wrath. My advice, may I add, has largely gone unheeded and her friendships are often 'on hold' until her indignation subsides.

Despite her complete lack of language, Daisy is a real people person. The guileless magnetism of her love draws friends like iron filings. In an effort to encourage Rosie and Lenny to get the most out of their schooldays, I have put in a lot of groundwork to support the building of their various friendships, but when it comes to Daisy, I am the novice, the eager student who has only learned real people skills through my careful observation of her methods. She offers her friendship freely and is unconcerned by any reciprocal benefits. It is this absolute, genuine and incorruptible affection for her fellow human beings that is Daisy's secret, I believe, and demonstrating such authenticity is something that cannot easily be learned and is impossible to fake.

Of the three siblings, Rosie and Lenny definitely have the closest relationship. They love to be together, pulling faces at one another, playing eye-contact games of which neither really understands the rules. They are very physical together, climbing on one another, spinning around, blowing 'raspberries' on one-another's bellies. I would guess that Rosie is Lenny's favourite person in the world, and it is a real joy to see them interacting so naturally, so often, and without a care between them of what the rest of the world thinks of their behaviour.

Daisy too loves her older sister. I believe she sees her as a source of fun, and also as someone who has the power to get her things (a mystic, an unlocker of doors, a fetcher of bananas, a runner of baths…).

Daisy and Lenny's relationship is far from harmonious. Loving the same toys, snacks and sensory stimulus, they recognise that for either one of them, the other is competition. In an effort to encourage spoken language, we often point to each family member on a photograph and prompt Lenny to say his or her name. 'Daddy, Mummy, Rosie, Lenny,' he will happily say, but when we point to Daisy the most we can procure is a disgusted 'D…'

A few years back, Lenny developed a fascination for tidying the living room. It was comical to see him running around, fast as a wind-up toy, placing cushions on sofas, books on bookshelves, and eliminating anything that he considered to be superfluous to his needs. One time he had thrown all of these unwanted items out of the door, and closed it firmly behind them, surveying his super-bare living quarters with anxious perfectionism. He then proceeded to bodily push Daisy from the room and slam the door after her. Job done. That just about sums up the bond that my younger two children share. It doesn't make me sad, though. On the contrary, that they have this very natural sibling rivalry is a source of great amusement to me. A hint of normality in an otherwise off-the-wall family.

I regularly organised tea parties for the children and their school friends when they were young. We would operate these parties on a three-week rota, one week we would have Rosie's friends, the following week Daisy's and on the third week it would be Lenny's turn to hand out the sticker-bedecked homemade invites. The parties weren't extravagant in any way, just a few sandwiches and sausage rolls, packets of crisps and a tray of home-baked buns. I probably enjoyed these 'friend-recruiting' teatimes as much as any of the children did. We would play Disney CDs, get out the dressing up box, do arts and crafts or sensory play. I would have my work cut out rounding up a satisfactory number of takers when it was Rosie or Lenny's turn to have friends round, but the merest suggestion that Daisy was hosting an 'open house' tea-party would have her school-friends chomping at the bit. Gradually, after much persistence, the return invites began to dribble in.

Because of the gradual adjustments that we had made over time, our home became virtually untrashable, but other families, it seemed, lived in much more tenuous circumstances. Ever hungry, Daisy would make a bee-line for party buffets, or snatch tempting food from other revellers' paper plates. With his deep aversion to clothing, we lived with the constant threat that Lenny might decide to perform an impromptu strip, or, after one too many beakers of blackcurrant, might feel the need to relieve himself on the bunting-strewn lawn. I was often the only parent opting to stick around, other mums and dads, having more manageable offspring, would drop their kids off and take the opportunity to go shopping or enjoy a couple of hour's peace and quiet. It was better if Richard could be with me to help to keep an eye on Daisy and Lenny, and to lend a hand cleaning up the inevitable devastation before we said our embarrassed goodbyes, but the parties were often directly after school time, drawing to their chaotic conclusion at around the time he returned from work. From a very young age, Rosie acted as my significant other at these events, explaining, managing, cleaning up with me. I would feel the weight of guilt that she wasn't completely free to enjoy the parties, and each time I would resolve not to call on her for help. Half an hour into the celebration, however, and I would be summoning her, asking her to keep an eye on one sibling while I changed the other, or prevent any more destruction while I put the last calamity to rights.

It was against everything that I believed in to decline invitations – how could our children ever hope to learn how to socialise, or to behave appropriately if they were not given the chance to experience the fun side of growing up? And anyway, what kind of childhood would that be, with no parties or discos to anticipate and enjoy? I devised a workable strategy. Assuring the parents of the birthday girl or boy in question that my children would love to attend, I would then claim to have a prior appointment, and would apologise in advance for the fact that we might well be late. Turning up for the last forty-five minutes of a two-hour party, my kids got to experience the best bit, the culmination of the revelry when the room was already warmed up. The lighting of the candles and the out of tune singing of 'happy birthday.' By this stage of the game, standards had often slipped dramatically. Party going children being as they are, the venue would often already be disordered, the buffet ransacked and most of the colourful balloons sagging or burst. Being fashionably late, we slotted beautifully into the chaos, party clothes fresh, and completely blameless for any crime that may have been committed before our arrival.

Party invites, or the fact that party invites are in short supply, may be a matter very close to your autism mum's heart. If you have the patience, and the inclination, then perhaps you could help her to organise and to supervise the occasional low-key get-together for her child and his friends, in order to pique his interest in the wonderful possibilities that socialisation holds. Party guests must have realistic expectations, though, and any activities can be built around her child's interests or obsessions. In this way, her little one is more likely to remain engaged throughout the occasion, and the invitees are able to get to know him a little better, to gain an insight into what makes him tick.

When, finally, her youngster receives his reciprocal invite, then you could offer your services and attend the party with the two of them. Support in these kind of situations is invaluable. One unsuccessful party could trigger years of unanswered invites, so it is vital that early socialising is well-supported and leaves Mum feeling a sense of achievement and child with an appetite for fun.

It's good to remember that friendships do not begin and end with people who are of a similar age. Over time, the relationship between you and your friend's child can also become a real and valuable friendship, and one that will benefit each of you accordingly.

As the years have gone on, I have relaxed, both with regard to my obsessive fear that the children's disruptive behaviour will cause offence, and in my relentless pursuit of friendship on their behalf. Their behaviour tends to sort the wheat from the chaff, and if our hosts are unbearably sniffy about a few crumbs, the odd puddle of wee or broken teacup, then these probably aren't the most useful people to have in our lives. I realise that the children's relationships with us, their parents, with one another, and with people outside of our family, are unique. I no longer nag Rosie to 'choose her battles' and constantly forgive the outrageously sexist comments that her young male friends frequently come out with. It was exhausting, smoothing over all of those spats. Anyway, it best serves the boys to unlearn their casual chauvinism. I've switched sides now and instead insist that guests to our home think carefully before carelessly offending any one of us, or for that matter causing offence to one another. Rosie is a change-maker, and if there is one thing that experience has taught me, it is that changes aren't usually forged through timidity and people pleasing.

As for Daisy and Lenny, any relationship with a normally developing peer is likely to involve much give and take, an element of care or support, a level of understanding or maturity that is out of the reach of many adults, never mind children. Any relationships between them and other children with disabilities will require the support of someone far more expert than me, someone who is familiar with both parties; namely teaching or respite staff. My strategy now is to allow nature to take its course. When young people are interested in the children, and actively want to include them, then, of course, I very much appreciate and welcome this. If their interest is more cautious, then I do my best to offer the kind of encouragement that will help them to consider people who are very different from them as potential friends. Just as parents of typically developing children must stand back and allow their children to make their own way in through the friendship jungle, then so, I have realised, must I.

Of course, we must be on guard to protect our vulnerable children, while still bearing in mind that all children are vulnerable, and that friendship is a gift to be treasured, rather than a mandatory requirement.

Personal Cares

As your friend's child gets older, there is every chance that the natural expansion of his sphere of relationships will be arrested because of the need for whoever is in charge to perform his personal cares. In the case of a typically developing child, the youngster is potty trained between the ages of two and three, and step-by-step, is able to take over the management of his own dressing, washing, and bathroom visits.

When a child has autism, development doesn't always follow this predictable path. Higher functioning children are often (but by no means always) able to develop these fundamental life-skills at the age appropriate time, leaving them free to spend nights with Grandma or Aunty, or to go for an after-school tea-party with their classmates.

When a five-year-old still wears nappies day and night or has to be laboriously taken through every nitty-gritty step of the way when toileting, this does not tend to do him any favours in the arena of social progression. Invites are few and far between for the smearer and the spitter or for the boy who habitually puts his hands down his trousers. You don't tend to get invited to tea if your food has to be mushed up and spoon-fed to you, or if you are apt to let it fall from your mouth to the carpeted floor if it is not to your liking. Frankly, you can hardly blame people, but we must learn to see these behaviours for what they are, purely an extension of the babyhood phase. Most people are not used to taking care of the personal needs of a child who has moved on from the toddling stage, and to many people, the very idea of it is distasteful.

The implications of this barrier are significant, both for the child and his mother. 'Natural respite' as I like to call it, happens gradually, organically. Girls tend to pair off with 'best friends' at the age of seven or eight, and spend much of their free time in each other's houses. Boys might traditionally hang out in gangs, but they will spend time away from the home attending scouts, football clubs or band practice. The child whose personal and learning cares prevent such progress also finds himself without the variety of social stimulation and learning experiences that enrich children's lives. No sleepovers, no Brownies, no karate or drama club. No best friend and no party invites. Surely, as a compassionate society, we can do better than this? If the child is aware of this difference between his social experience and that of his peers, then he is likely to feel most dissatisfied with his lot. He is more than likely to blame his difference, his disability, and begin to look upon it as a significantly negative thing.

For Mum, the implications are dreadful. Not only must she perform all of these extra tasks for her child, but she must do it alone. When the average mum starts to see the light at the end of the babyhood tunnel, the autism mum continues to plod along in the dark. I noticed in the children's pre-teenage years that many of my friends were beginning to claw back the fun elements of their lives. They were going back to work, or, in some cases, even starting new careers. I watched on as they enjoyed regular nights out with their husbands or friends, while their children had a weekend with the grandparents. This was just not happening for me. Not only did I find that I was unable to reclaim my pre-pregnancy life, but the general trend of my daily labour was that things were becoming increasingly difficult. There were at least three loads of washing to do each day; Daisy and Lenny became so messy that even their coats need to be laundered on a daily basis. Even if I had the presence of mind to tie on aprons, drape them with napkins or pegged-round-the-neck tea towels at every meal or snacktime, they both dribbled profusely. And the laundry went further than clothes; bedding needed to be changed every morning, my own clothes would be covered in jammy or porridgy smears by midday. The hoover was constantly at hand; tasks that other people tended to do once in a blue moon were a three times a day affair for me. And still the place looked like the aftermath of a chimp's tea-party for most of the time.

Ever the optimist, I started to get up earlier and earlier in order to get ahead, to put the first wash on, prepare food for the day and make the place look like a stark approximation of other people's houses. Daisy and Lenny seemed to follow my lead, and spent more of their time awake than asleep. The slightest noise would wake them. As soon as they were up and about, I had to spend my waking moments supervising, dressing, washing, changing and generally keeping them out of trouble.

The more time that I spent on these dreary household tasks, the less time I had for spending essential learning time and even more essential fun time with my children. It seemed that I was on a treadmill, and that whatever malevolent force was operating the controls of this device, the only plan was to increase the resistance as my children became bigger, stronger and more determined to fulfill their sensory desires.

It was suggested to me that unless I got some extra help with the children, I would go under. At first, I refused to even consider respite care. Stubbornly, heroically, I would continue. Despite the harsh regime of my working day, I would turn it up a gear. I would become Supermum. They were my children, and whatever needed to be done on their behalf, then the task should fall to me.

Of course, this attitude was foolish and unrealistic. I see now that the mothers of the typical children in our community weren't doing everything by themselves, they were gradually beginning to depend on the wider web of care that is spun by Aunties, best friend's mothers, grandparents and community groups. My children were either at school, or they were with me. Something had to give.

Eventually I went to take a look at a local respite resource, and it didn't take me very long at all to realise that I was not the only one who would benefit from the extra help. Typically, children with moderate or severe learning disabilities attended this placement for three overnight sessions each month. They were collected at the end of their school day (either one of the special educational settings in our area or from mainstream school). They were brought back for tea, allowed to choose their own room, often taken out on the bus for a visit, and then back for a bit of TV or crafting before bed. I quickly realised that it wasn't a case of these kids being dumped so that their parents could enjoy a bit of child-free time; the children were having fun! They were well cared for, well stimulated and they were being offered an opportunity to socialise within a carefully matched group of peers. They were being offered variety, tea-parties, the chance to do all of the things that typical children were doing in their after-school lives.

Not only that, but the staff were not the slightest bit squeamish about changing nappies, supervising baths, cleaning teeth, dressing and tidying up after the children. This was their chosen profession! Further, because of the extensive experience working with young people and the regular training that they were required to undergo, they would be able to offer advice and practical help with moving the children on from their very dependent state.

Things moved pretty quickly after that. It was decided that Daisy and Lenny would first attend the resource for a tea visit, with me present, so that staff could get to know them. A week after this tea visit, they would be able to spend their first overnight session there. Apart from Daisy's frequent hospital stays (when I was always there, on the pull-down bed or snoozing in the chair by her side) neither of them had ever spent a night away from us.

I clearly remember that first night that they stayed away from home. I had been able to get the house straight during the daytime while Daisy and Lenny were at school. Instead of sitting around the formal dining table for dinner, we pulled out a coffee table in front of the TV in the living room, brought out plates of crackers, ham and cheese, and Richard, Rosie and I ate our dinner watching a movie, just like a normal family! It was eerily quiet that night, and the next morning, so strange to get up, take a leisurely bath, spend time dressing and applying make-up, instead of my usual routine of a ninety-second shower and an ungainly leap into my jeans and t-shirt.

Respite works well for us. Moreover, I would say, it is essential. Whenever the children are home, we do our very best to make sure that something happens for them every night. Unable as they are to entertain themselves, they need direction and organisation. In the summer, we picnic at one of our local parks, but the winter time is more tricky. We swim, go for fish and chips, or wander around late-night shopping centres. Stuck in the house, the children become very unhappy. The extra help that we get from respite services enables us to step down a gear once in a while, to do age appropriate things with Rosie (cinema visits, board games, or, as on that very first respite night, curl up on the sofa and watching a movie together). If we have the energy, it means that Richard and I also get a little time to have dinner or a drink together, to invest in the relationship that forms the central core of our children's lives.

I hope your autism mum will consider accessing help from respite services. Maybe you could suggest accompanying her on a visit to her local resource, so that she can see for herself what a wonderful source of support these centres provide for children with additional needs and their families.

If you are the resilient type, with a no-nonsense attitude towards toileting and intimate care, then perhaps you could have a frank discussion with her about what lengths you are prepared to go to in order for her to enjoy the occasional afternoon or evening to herself. God knows, performing such tasks is not everyone's cup of tea, and I know from experience that helping our own children to stay clean and hygienic and giving the same assistance to someone else's are two very different matters. If you are willing and able, though, and if your friend knows that she can entrust her precious little one to your expert care, then please make yourself available once in a while. You have no idea how deeply your devoted dedication will be valued.

The Things That People Say

I could probably write a whole book cataloguing the reactions that I've had to my family, but I'm happy to condense the highlights and the lowlights into a single chapter. This may help you understand; if your friend is sometimes angry at the world, bemused or overwhelmed by the things that people do and say – she may have good reason. My hope, though, is that you can be on hand to re-focus her attention – for every one negative reaction that I receive about my family, there are ten encouraging responses. It's far too easy to become entrenched in the murk of this life, and to ignore the abundance of cheerful optimism that surrounds us. I believe that the onus is on us; which way to look? To which version of truth shall we nod our acceptance? This is our own personal choice.

A good place to begin, when considering the pain that bigoted opinions and comments can wreak, is to remind ourselves that the opinion of the majority is not necessarily right. I revisit this fact on a daily basis, constantly checking that my ideas and reactions to events are genuine, and that they are truly my own. The temptation to look to others, to gauge what is acceptable by the reaction of the majority, can be strong, but ultimately, I believe that to hand over the shaping of our values to the majority is a lazy and dangerous practice. There was a time when the majority opinion was that this earth was as flat as a pancake. The few original thinkers who opposed this consensus were ridiculed, supposed insane.

Out and about in society, with my unusual family in tow, I am met with all manner of feedback, some of which comes in the form of glowers and glares from individuals who I am sure base their hostility on an unclear feeling that something is 'not quite right.'

In the early days, this reaction used to completely floor me. My counter-reaction to the vague hostility? To cower, to return to the safety of my home, to wonder what on earth I had done wrong to invite such constant punishment. Of course, time has added the weight of confidence to my responses, and now I meet hostility head on, or, even more effectively, with a reassuring smile and an invitation to get to know my extraordinary little family, to learn something from the encounter.

When the children were very young, only the fact that Daisy was pushed along in her wheelchair provided the casual observer with any clue to the fact that ours might not be the average family. It probably took a little more interaction with us as a group to ascertain that we were about as far away from the 'normal' mark as it was possible to get. But that's OK, to quote the famous wisdom of my eldest daughter 'What's so great about 'normal'?'

Until about the age of five, Lenny, prince like and aloft of danger, would be carried along on the shoulders of the parent who was not pushing Daisy's wheelchair at the time. I developed a swift, one-motion lift to avoid the frequent and ungainly scramble up my back. Lenny would stand in front of me, arms held high to indicate his desire to be elevated to his rightful throne. I would scoop my son up, my hands securely around his waist, lifting him up and back, over my head, where he would settle comfortably on his human perch. I have so many photographs of this period of his development, and in many I am holding Lenny's legs securely across my torso with one arm, while pushing Daisy's wheelchair with my other. Nothing notably out of the ordinary here, I guess, many young children enjoy the occasional shoulder ride if their parents are physically up to the job. With hindsight, though, this habit of carrying him on our shoulders probably gave him his love of nesting in high places and appreciating the birds-eye view of his environment that would cause us no end of problems in years to come. Still, you live and learn.

As the years went by, though, Lenny became too large for his preferred mode of transport. I remember filling in a lengthy form when applying for a double Major McLaren buggy (two large ones bolted together for our very specific purposes). In one box I was asked to explain 'why do you feel that you should be entitled to a grant for this item?' I sassily replied 'to prevent my spine from crumbling.' Sarcasm is the lowest form of wit, and often irritates the very people who we need to help us. Still, it's lots of fun.

We got the grant, but the supersize double buggy wasn't the easiest thing to handle, pushing it plus the combined weight of Daisy and Lenny, with arms always held akimbo because of the sheer breadth of the thing, was a hard task that I adapted to over time. There are usually secondary gains to any situation, and I developed amazing upper arm tone. In those days, no end of take-away food or packets of biscuits would leave their wobbly mark on my body.

I'm sure we made an impact as we travelled along with our supersized adapted wheels. Rosie, still waiting for her own diagnosis, would delight in feeding interested strangers random snippets of information about our family. A real chatterbox, she loved to strike up conversations with all manner of people, regardless of any reciprocal interest.

'This is my little brother, Lenny, we call him Len-Lens for short, even though it's longer. That's an irony as well because he is the biggest but also the youngest. He likes to spin and to jump because of his autism. He doesn't like his chicken dippers anywhere near his blob of ketchup because that makes him sick, and I agree. And this is my little sister Daisy, who has Kabuki Syndrome. That's very rare, she's one in a million. You can probably see, she's small for her age but beautiful as an angel! Once she walked seventeen steps at the Old Mill, so we made posters to celebrate and stuck them in the windows. Kabuki Syndrome isn't great though because it makes her get sick a lot, and Daisy and Mum go to hospital, so Dad gets to look after us then.'

'And what about you?' asked an interested observer on one memorable occasion, in response to Rosie's bombardment of information. 'What do you have?'

'Oh, I have constipation,' Rosie replied breezily, before moving on to her next victim. It transpired later that this lady helped to deliver the National Autistic Society's 'Early Bird' programme, a parenting course for mums and dads with newly diagnosed children. Anne-Marie was clearly in the know, and was quick to recognise the tell-tale quirkiness in my eldest daughter. I've since become involved in the running of the Early Bird course (and, if the course is running in her area, would highly recommend that your friend consider enrolling). I've helped out with the delivery of a few of their sessions now, and the time-worn anecdote of pre-diagnosis Rosie and her constipation is a story that beautifully illustrates the enchanting quirkiness of the autist. Also, it gets a laugh every time.

My eldest certainly saved me a lot trouble and explanation in those days. Having Rosie on hand with her never-ending stream of banter was a source of entertainment for us, as well as being a source of extemporised information for the world at large. Occasionally, I would smile and nod by way of backing up her improbable tales, but for the most part I would simply stand back and enjoy the show.

Nowadays, if the children are not with me and I chance to strike up a conversation with a stranger, when the talk turns to family and young children (as it always seems to, eventually), I get the uncomfortable feeling that people might find my story a little unlikely. I recognise the familiar shadow of uncertainty – is this woman exaggerating? Either that or she is an out and out fantasist! Oh-oh, Munchausen's by Proxy alert!

Let me take you through a hypothetical conversation by way of example. Picture me walking through our friendly little village, popping into the local shops for a bit of light shopping. A fellow shopper mentions that the footpaths in the village are in a shocking state, they seem to become narrower every year. She reflects that it must cause a lot of problems for people using wheelchairs or prams.

I agree wholeheartedly. I mention that my daughter is a wheelchair user, and that it can be a real struggle to stay safely off the road when the paths become so narrow. Then comes the question about the nature of Daisy's disability, followed by my succinct explanation. The fact that she uses a wheelchair is more to do with her limited learning ability than anything physical. She often goes on strike, slumping to the ground like a bag of sand if she's unwilling to go any further. She's fifteen now, so even if she were willing to be carried, I wouldn't have the muscle power.

Oh dear, the stranger shakes her head, that must be difficult. After a pensive moment, she might go on to reassure me that there are worse things than having a child with a learning disability. She may mention that she has heard a lot about autism in the media recently, and these children can be incredibly difficult to love, almost impossible to care for.

I know a bit about autism, I answer, my son was diagnosed at three. He may be a lot of things, but he is certainly loveable. He can be very tricky, but he brings me lots of joy. I never go short of cuddles!

My new friend narrows her eyes suspiciously. Two children? Different conditions? After careful consideration, she may conclude that I have a genuine case, and go on to reassure me that my son might grow out of this 'autism' that's all the rage these days. She's heard that some people with the condition can grow up to be ever so capable, a few even becoming geniuses, like that Bill Gates chap or Einstein.

Yes, I know, I have one of those as well! I might say. Or I may just smile and go on my way, quitting while I am ahead. When wrapped up in the conversational nutshell of a few exchanged pleasantries, our story seems so unlikely.

Although I love chatting to people, and find no subject more thoroughly engaging than that of my own family, when you don't know the background or the level of understanding that a person has, any conversations can become a Russian Roulette situation. Although a good proportion of the people I speak to are fairly knowledgeable, and are easily taught that autism is not the condition from hell that it used to be sold as, I have been asked many direct and hurtful questions over the years. I see now that this is part and parcel of the general learning trend that has swept our society over the past ten years. People need to ask, if they are to learn. Some of the questions, though, were incredibly hurtful.

For example, 'Are you and your husband cousins, or something?' Er, no. We most certainly are not.

In high school one particularly unpleasant young girl took it upon herself to inform Rosie that her younger siblings were 'like that' because her parents took drugs. Rosie was quiet when she came home from school that day, pale and withdrawn. The harder I tried to coax her to share the reason for her troubled mood with me, the further away from me she shrank. Eventually she broke down and told me what the girl had said. Children don't generally have the guile to spread such poison, and I strongly suspected that this cruel accusation had come via the girl from her parents. Drugs? No. I do chomp my way through numerous packs of Rennies each month, but my flirtation with narcotics begins and ends there.

The saddest reaction that I regularly receive to my children's conditions is the pitying, forlorn headshake.

'It's such a shame,' the pity-mongers mope, patting Daisy's curly mop, lost in the mistaken belief that this condescending behaviour is somehow akin to kindness. My heart sinks to the bottom of my boots – I'm filled with a bleak gloom that can last for the rest of the day, or until I decide to 'woman-up' and shake it off. Nothing about my children could ever be connected with shame, my shame, their shame – the only shame that I see is for a society rendered blind by preconceptions.

In the supermarket one time; Lenny, chomping through a bag of chocolate buttons, played an interesting game of trying to physically hold back the conveyor belt with the palm of his sturdy hand as I packed our groceries. A chap who had been ahead of us in the queue was hanging back, watching Lenny, fascinated by his interest in the conveyor belt. This man clearly had a mild learning disability, and perhaps recognised a kindred spirit in Lenny.

'He's a right lad, in't he?' he said to me, by way of compliment. 'What's your name, then, feller? Are you helping your mum? He's a right lad. A smasher!'

Lenny was grinning from ear to ear, basking in the positive attention, but when the man eventually left with his trolley, I was horrified to find the cashier rolling her eyes and making a 'screw loose' gesture with her hand.

'He's talking about your lad, but he's just as bad!' she said to me, with a derisive snigger. The assumption that this might be an acceptable thing to say took me aback, robbed me of any response. I said nothing, but summoned up my most disconcerting, laser-eyed stare. She took my payment and I left without a thank you.

Later that day, though, reflecting on the supermarket incident, I had to have a word with myself. I expect tolerance, and I expect my children to be loved and embraced, valued for their own sake, for who they are, regardless of their learning disabilities or their sometimes disruptive behaviour. I came to a decision that maybe I should practice what I preach, and afford tolerance to people who may simply have outdated attitudes. If we are all on a path towards enlightenment, then there will be many hundreds of thousands of people who are behind me on that path, as well as the few dozen who are ahead of me (haha). I realised that there are many people who have not had the benefit of my life experience to aid the evolution of their understanding. And then there are people who, for want of a better expression, are just a bit dim.

These people must be given a leg up towards better understanding, rather than be punished for their lack of life experience. Of course, we have on occasion met with people who are just plain nasty. The bullies of this world who will see difference and attack. One evening, returning from our local shop with a bag of groceries, I noticed a man, a father with two young girls, of perhaps six and eight years old. They seemed to be gesturing towards our house and I wondered what the matter might be. I approached, ready to ask if they needed help when I heard the man say to his daughters 'Shall we look for the monsters, can you see them, look through the window?'

This man knew that I was there, witness to his unfathomably cruel words. He looked me straight in the eye and then began to sing the theme tune to *The Addams Family* to his little daughters, who laughed along, innocent of their daddy's viciousness. This episode left me physically ill, I made it to the bathroom before vomiting. Unable to rationalise the concept that a grown man could possibly be so heartless, Richard reasoned that I must have got the wrong end of the stick. I knew what I had seen and what I had heard, however, and nothing had ever hurt me so deeply before, and never has since. After this unpleasantness, I became quite paranoid about people walking past the house and very protective of who could see in. I encouraged the children to do their evening activities at the back of the house, in the dining room where no passers-by could see in. For the front room, I had commissioned full black out blinds, and had them turned down at all times, day and night. I see now that this was an overreaction, a definite mental health wobble on my behalf. I'm happy to report that I got over the incident eventually, dispensed with the blinds and allowed the light of the world back it our front room and our lives.

On a summer's evening at our local park, Daisy and Lenny love nothing better than to sit amid a circle of gravel which provides a fall-break for a giant tyre swing. It's their favourite spot in the world, and we have spent many serene hours languishing here. I recently told Richard and Rosie that this is the spot that I choose for my ashes to be scattered after my demise, as it is the place where, in my adult life, I have felt most contented. Granted, the gravel beneath a tyre swing in a children's playground is not a traditionally sacred spot like Stonehenge. It isn't bleak and hauntingly beautiful, like the Yorkshire Moors. For me, though, any location where my younger two will sit, engaged, content not to wander off in different directions and allow me a little time to read my book or relax, attains a certain divine ambience.

Here, Daisy and Lenny are able to freely indulge their sensory natures, repeatedly scooping up handfuls of the stones, and then letting them fall to the ground. Little clouds of grey dust float dreamily in the shards of evening sunlight. Delicious, sensory heaven for my children. With the apricot glow of the setting sun, the gentle breath of the breeze chasing dandelion seeds and dust motes, here we sit surrounded by the timeless sounds of birdsong and playing children. For a few hours, our troubles are weightless and we truly are in paradise.

Rose and I will sit on the grass alongside Daisy and Lenny, drinking coffee from a flask and chatting about our day. Very young children and toddlers are often drawn to the spectacle of my youngest two children's sensory play. Sifting the evening away in a state near spiritual bliss, hypnotised by the magic of the stones. The little ones watch for a while, and inevitably join in, keen to try out this happy activity for themselves. When they try it, they love it!

Well-adjusted parents tend to let them get on with it. Elbow deep in dirt is the best way for children to experience childhood, in my humble opinion.

One time, though, a young mum in neatly ironed lemon cardigan and other spotless attire yanked her toddler away by the arm.

'Get OUT of that dirt!' she yelled at her startled daughter.

'But they're doing it!' protested the youngster.

'Well their mummy is a very silly mummy and she should tell them to stop!'

There was, indeed, one very silly mummy in the park that day, but I can say with confidence that it wasn't me.

I have heard the words 'Don't even look!' hissed at curious children who have been watching on, fascinated by Daisy and Lenny's behaviour. Imagine the implication. For an innocent child, maybe this is their first ever encounter with a learning disabled person, and they are reprimanded in such a harsh way, 'Don't even look!' What a perfectly concise way to set the scene for a lifetime of fear and mistrust. Sometimes, I despair. If parents were only to become conscious of the way that their attitudes are passed directly to their children, a blueprint of learned behaviour, then perhaps they would think a little more carefully before letting such damaging words do their detrimental work.

A preferable, much more desirable, reaction would go so much further towards supporting understanding, curiosity and empathy. When 'Don't even look!' becomes 'Let's go and say "hello"' then we have the level foundation on which to build something beautiful.

Please don't worry for me, I am fully reconciled to these occasional negative reactions now. In fact, because of the positive attitude that I have been forced to adapt in order to do the best possible job that I can in raising my children, I now see these infrequent episodes of animosity as timely reminders. My job is far from completion. While ever these antagonistic remnants of a bitter bygone age are still among us, these dark pockets of nastiness that we stumble upon from time to time, there is still work to be done. No resting on the proverbial laurels for me!

When people tell me that my family is unacceptable, either with their words, their shifty sideways on looks, or by their refusal to let their own children come near us, then I faithfully return to my own appraisal of our reality. We are incredibly strong in our love for one another. My children are enchanting and astonishing. They are blessed with their own individual natures, and have many wonderful skills and unique personality traits. The world is round; nay, spherical!

And yet, here I am lamenting, focusing on the negative, when I have witnessed so many delightful and delighted reactions to my family. Since the story of Rosie's self-diagnosis made it on to the local news some eight or nine years ago, there have been a handful of short films made about the Kings. Once the media snowball started rolling down the hill, there seemed no stopping it. All kinds of people were asking us to do television interviews, radio, to talk within schools, colleges and other organisations. Others told me that they considered us to be very brave, embracing and welcoming the media's interest in this way. I've come full circle since the days when I hid behind the blackout blinds for fear of outside aggression. From my point of view, our decision to 'let the cameras in' is only an extension of the way that we let the general public in all of the time, opening up lines of communication, illustrating in no uncertain terms that it is fine for people to look, to ask questions, and ultimately to learn from us.

I welcome any opportunity to teach, and to learn. It has to be said, though, that the more that I learn about autism, the more I realise I am right at the beginning of my journey of discovery. If anyone tells you that they are an autism expert, you have my permission to remain sceptical. It's an elusive subject, slippery as a shadow. Even if we are willing and able to grasp the fundamentals, we soon meet another person with the condition who blows our understanding out of the water. Our understanding of this condition changes constantly. We must continuously empty ourselves of preconceptions, in order to be in the best position to learn.

With regards to the media and public speaking that we are involved in, I feel incredibly grateful that we have been given access to a platform from which to spread our message of positivity. However much the media is scorned in our society, television is, in fact, the best and most direct way to furnish the greatest number of people with the most up to date and immediate information.

As a result of the good news slant on our lives that we have chosen to broadcast, letters, photographs and stories, messages of support and warmth come back to us from all over the globe. These messages come directly from other people who are affected by autism and by other disabilities or differences. We are often contacted by parents, siblings, teachers and friends of autists. We are asked questions and we are asked for advice. We are often given valuable advice in return. These communications are the proof that I need to be sure that the world in which we live is gradually changing for the better. They are what keeps me smiling after a particularly upsetting encounter. When I receive an email from a struggling mother somewhere else on the planet in which she tells me that my bloody-minded refusal to go under and to stick to my positive stance has had a beneficial effect on her, this buoys me up and makes me even more determined. I remember that, even though change can never be instantaneous, our attitude towards disability is evolving all the time.

My son Christopher is also on the spectrum, PDD. He obsesses with Minions from *Despicable Me* and also loves...no...ADORES penguins. His neurologist has said that he may be high functioning as time passes. If this is true, I rejoice, but however it happens, we love him beyond words and celebrate his uniqueness.

Thank you for this beautifully refreshing reminder that it is often the daily, simple and easily accessible moments of shared joy that enlivens us where we really need or long for it. Fingers running through rice or sand, smelling the heady scent of gardenia or the

freshness of paint. Life, love and laughter are all about us, if we have eyes and hearts to see. Again, thank you.

Yours is truly a Home, meaning each of you knows you are accepted for who you are with a mountain of Love and Encouragement. There is nothing bleak about your home, only space to bloom into Self. Fabulous family, more power to you.

I stumbled across your TEDMED talk. I watched it with my 11-year-old son, who has Asperger's. A couple of times during the video I heard him say 'I am just like her!' I've never heard him connect on that kind of level with anyone. I just wanted to say thank you for sharing your lives and experiences.

So, I'm 19 and have recently been diagnosed with autism and yourself and your daughter Rosie have inspired me so much with facing it, accepting it, and trying not to act like it doesn't exist. So, I'd like to say thank you to you and Rosie for being an upfront and honest set of people.

Hi, I watched your *Newsround* programme when I was first diagnosed with autism in 2013 and I could really relate, especially when you said like how you feel inanimate objects like your shoes have emotions. Then I found your TED talk a few years later and it was just so good. I'm so happy to have found you.

I like your blue hair.

I'm so glad that you've found ways to overcome whatever new challenge may turn up on life's journey. I have struggled at every stage in life from problem child to problem teenager, to problem adult. How could it have been any different being at school in the '50s and '60s? I was finally diagnosed at age 65. Autism, Asperger's, Chronic Anxiety and later Misophonia. Many people struggle in retirement, so I was determined to write my life's story of struggle in my first winter of retirement. Thank you for being brave, Rosie. I have learned a lot from you.

These far flung responses represent the wider influence that we are able to effect in the world, but closer to home, we are finding that every encounter can be subtly manipulated to provide a learning experience for everyone involved.

When we eat out in a restaurant, we like to give people close by fair warning.

Our kids can be noisy and messy. It has to be said that the family is a little chaotic. Richard, Rosie and I make a point of opening up the conversation and assuring people sitting near us that it is fine for them to switch tables if they're keen to enjoy a peaceful meal. After all, regardless of our needs and challenges, these people are paying good money to enjoy an evening away from whatever challenges they might face in their own lives. It's good for us to remind ourselves that even when people aren't facing the same kind of difficulties as we are, each and every human being is making their way over the constant assault course that is life. They're entitled to a peaceful dinner every now and then.

As yet, however, nobody has ever taken us up on our invitation to move away from our table. Not even once. Our genuine offer would make it easy for someone to switch tables with no offence given and none taken, with no recriminations for either party. That our offer is always cheerfully declined strengthens my faith in humanity. If anything, our polite forewarning tends to recruit allies. Because of our peace-making initiative, a conversation is kicked off and is usually followed up by a gentle enquiry about the children, how old are they? Where do they go to school? Sometimes the conversation ends here, and our new friends carry on with their meal. Of course, that is OK. On many occasions, though, the conversation takes on a life of its own, takes all parties involved to a deeper level of understanding. We are able to positively influence our new friends, or we are able to learn from their experience. The situation is skilfully swayed, and we find that we can easily create an opportunity for friendship and mutual learning. This group exploration of facts, ideas and attitudes is infinitely preferable to a hostile stand-off, built on misinformation and mistrust.

Time after time, we find that most people want to be tolerant, they are actually very keen to push the boundaries of their understanding. With our no-nonsense frankness, we find that we are able to bring light to the dark and scary corners of people's perception. History is littered with horrible examples, illustrating our innate tendency to fear and attack anything that we do not understand. That this is a primitive survival instinct can no longer be an excuse. We are primitives no more; we have come far enough along the evolutionary yardstick to be fully aware that difference is not threat. More; difference and diversity are essential for a healthy, dynamic society.

When there is accurate knowledge available, and this is coupled with a willingness to learn, there is no place left for fear or apprehension.

'May I say, your children have been remarkably well-behaved,' an elderly and quite well-to-do lady congratulated us as she put on her coat to leave a restaurant where we had all been enjoying a noisy, disorganised dinner. I glanced at the food spillages on the floor, the debris caused by the half packet of wet-wipes which we had used to mop up. I am often told that my children are 'beautiful,' that they are 'sweet,' or 'real characters'. 'Well-behaved,' however, is a phrase not so often bandied about. I couldn't help but fleetingly wonder whether she was being sarcastic. A direct look into her faded-denim-blue eyes, though, and I could see that this well-mannered lady recognised our struggles. It was impossible to guess where her insight might have come from, but she clearly saw that, for our kids, to sit down for the hour and a half long duration of a three course meal was an accomplishment in itself. I basked in the glow of her words throughout dessert. It could have been the three glasses of merlot that I'd quaffed with my meal, but I like to think that we made a little connection. Never underestimate the power of a sincere, dignified compliment!

The words that we use to describe people with learning disabilities keep changing. Every generation or so a new, fashionable, politically correct term is ushered in, and the old words superseded, banned. This endless race to remain one step ahead of those who use our descriptions of differently abled people to mock or as an insult will have to continue. Even the phrase 'special needs' is used as an insult now. We will be forced to escape the echoes of the bullies' words by constantly changing the way that we refer to those of us with learning disabilities until the fundamental attitudes are changed. When we no longer feel the need to mock our disabled brothers and sisters, we will be free to use descriptions that carry no negativity. Words change all of the time, people who are not abreast of the most modern lingo often get things wrong. I have met people who swoop on these casual mistakes, making an embarrassed example out of whoever has erroneously used an obsolete term. I hope to be more forgiving, realising as I do that the words are not nearly so important as the sentiment that lies beneath them. If there is no harm meant, then my practice is simply to repeat what was said, but to replace the outmoded label with whatever the new, socially acceptable one happens to be. New lamps for old, a fair exchange.

People sometimes say the wrong things. People often say the right things, and sometimes people say things that are downright hilarious. The important thing is to keep the conversations going. Points of view that I consider to be 'wrong' can be challenged or put back on track, if we have the opportunity to talk to people. How can we ever expect anyone to even begin to learn, or to eventually understand, if they feel that they shouldn't 'even look'?

A pair of ten-year-old girls, best friends and next door neighbours, as they informed me, once took a keen interest in Daisy and Lenny at the local library. As usual, we were creating a bit of a spectacle. At that time Lenny's destructive passion was to sweep the contents of the bookshelves to the library floor time and time again. He seemed to find the fluttering of the old, musty smelling pages delightfully amusing. No end of stern 'No, Lenny's!' would sway him from his destruction and the librarian was less than impressed by his antics. The two girls were helpfully assisting me in my endless task of returning the hardbacks to their allotted places.

These charming girls were full of the frank, direct questions that I find so refreshing. They were genuinely interested. Why did Daisy wear ankle splints? What did Lenny like to eat for his tea? Did the children use sign language? No? Then why didn't I teach them? Did they go to school, and, if so, did they get homework? How were their bedrooms decorated?

Used to dealing with adults who often edge their way cautiously around any conversations that they find difficult or embarrassing, I found this free-flowing Q&A session most agreeable.

'Do Daisy and Lenny have any other brothers and sisters?' one of the girls asked.

'Yes, they have a big sister, Rosie. She's sixteen.'

'And is she like them, or is she human?' There elapsed a couple of moments of horrified silence while the girls weighed up the implication of these words. Two pairs of wide eyes were fixed firmly on me as I processed the question, and tried to formulate a suitable reply.

No reply came, but I laughed until my sides ached!

Getting Practical

I'm very much hoping that if you have bought this book then you are after a little more than vague theories or examples of how difficult/wonderful life can be when you have a little autist in your life. I am guessing that you want real, practical ideas about how you can support your friend. Because you love her, you want to make her life a little easier.

Firstly, may I assure you that you can make a difference. No problem is so great, so deep or so wide that the attention of a friend will make no impact at all. From your friend's point of view, even knowing that you care, that you recognise the fact that she is going through a very tough time and are prepared to take ten minutes out of your day to phone her, or to send her a message of support is a valuable starting point.

If you have the time and the inclination to take further steps towards supporting her, then there are lots and lots of ways that you can provide solid, practical help.

As I previously mentioned, social isolation is cited as one of the most difficult aspects of being the parent of an autistic child. One by one, and for a variety of reasons, friendships can die off. The fault does not always lie at the foot of her friends. Newly diagnosed mums can be unpredictable and protective. I should know. They are wont to lash out at those who are close to them. They are very likely to be unreasonable if someone makes an ill-judged comment, if they feel that they, or their child are being excluded in anyway, two and two can easily add up to twenty-two. Two hundred and twenty-two when we are feeling deeply paranoid. Be extra tolerant of your friend at this time. If she becomes accusatory or touchy, take the time to reassure, to explain any motives, go out of your way to actively heal the wounds of small disagreements before they start to fester and threaten the foundations of your friendship.

When we are bereaved, numb with grief and do not know which way to turn, people who are unfamiliar with the grieving process become embarrassed in our presence. They avoid us, considering themselves ill-equipped to deal with such raw emotion. They can worry about saying the wrong thing, or about not being able to say anything of value at all. The same is true of people's reaction when our children are newly diagnosed. We sense a definite withdrawing, and this is easy to understand, given that our friends and family are being ultra-careful not to offend. What our friends say to us hardly matters at all though. When we are in a state of shock, or going through a grieving process, we actually remember very little in the way of detail; who said which words and when. What we do remember is the way that people made us feel. Resolve to be there for your friend at this difficult time, try not to worry too much about the words that you choose to communicate your love and care, because they hardly matter at all.

This lamentable social isolation simply need not happen. It may well be the worst thing that your friend has to cope with, but it is also the most easily remedied. In my circle of friends and acquaintances I hear time and time again that it is not the children that are the problem, the autism itself is not the reason why people fall into the black hole of depression and feel that they can no longer cope. The real problem is society's inflexibility, that stubborn inability to accept and accommodate. Society, though, is never really the huge nameless force that we conveniently call 'them,' the powers that be and the unstoppable forces of discrimination and ideology. No. Society is only ever really you and me. When each one of us accepts responsibility for our own thoughts and actions, then this frightening, powerful sea that is 'society' soon breaks down into much more manageable, much more human-sized portions.

Despite Lenny's passion for the great outdoors, the combination of the British weather and Daisy's predisposition to chest infections has meant in the past that there have been times when I have been confined to the house – when I couldn't think of a single place to take the kids. Or at least, I couldn't think of a single place where I could anticipate a genuine welcome.

I've always been a bit of a home-bird, and, let's face it, who doesn't love a duvet day? We hole up inside, shaking our heads at the bitter weather conditions outside. But when you have one child crying constantly, feeling ill and miserable and letting you know about it in no uncertain terms, another becoming anxious and increasingly frustrated with the same old boring environment, and a third becoming upset by the constant crying, and picking up on your own stress levels, the situation is far from enjoyable. It's a recipe for distress. The situation is made all the more frustrating by the harsh truth that even if you could summon the energy to calm everyone down, wrap them up in protective layers of hats, coats, scarves and gloves, and pack the appropriate necessities, then once you venture out into the wider world, you may be faced with the harsh fact that there is nowhere to go.

Over the years our home has gradually been customised to make all of our lives easier.

Locks appeared on the kitchen and bathroom doors to prevent flooding about ten years ago (Lenny loves the trickle and gush of flowing water. Taps hold an alluring promise that is impossible for him to resist, the biscuit tin beckons constantly, bags of sugar and flour and packets of cereals long to be sprinkled over the floor, and that gas hob! The magical wonders of the silent blue flame...). Decoration is kept to a minimum. Matching paint pots are always at hand to repair the scratches and scrapes that appear on our walls on a daily basis. I love fresh flowers but, splashing out on the occasional fragrant bunch, I absolutely accept that sometime over the next few days I will enter the room to find the plastic vase tipped up and my deflowered blooms robbed of their delicate petals.

In order that the place doesn't look like an institution, or prison, we have lots of family photographs and home produced paintings, all displayed in wooden frames with no glass to preserve them into antiquity. Much of our furniture is screwed to the floor, to prevent Lenny from using the sofas, chairs and tables as giant building blocks (his most favourite activity). Our windows are screwed down, able only to let in an inch or so of fresh air, a gap through which even the most determined escapee could not slither. Alarm systems have been installed on front and back doors. When at home, I wear a plastic bracelet which vibrates to alert me when either the front or back doors are opened, so that I am able to swiftly check that the person entering or leaving is legitimately allowed to do so.

In short, our home and living circumstances are so customised in accordance with the children's needs that it is very difficult to relax in anyone else's. At home we are able to let down our guard a little. We have to keep one eye firmly on them though, because Daisy and Lenny are constantly discovering new ways to get into trouble. However hard we might try, our little mischief makers are always three steps ahead of us.

During visits to family or friends, I am constantly on high alert, watching as the children enthusiastically explore the new environment, searching for goodies, to sprinkle, spread, or to eat. In their defence, I have rarely analysed any behaviour of Daisy or Lenny's and concluded that badness was their intent. They really are not naughty children at all. The core motivation is always, always sensory gratification, and that need to explore and to stimulate their senses overrides any other consideration.

It wasn't always quite as difficult as it is now. Though the children have always been very sensory and inclined to tip things up and empty things out, as they have grown, so has their cunning. Daisy and Lenny tend to work as a team, and their desire for sensory gratification trumps any desire to do my bidding. The temptation is simply overwhelming. Would you ask a hungry dog to sit down next to a plate of roast beef and have it refrain from bolting the lot? This analogy is the nearest I can come to describing my children's overpowering craving for the physical fulfillment that they achieve through the sprinkling, smearing, scattering and splashing activities that get us into constant trouble.

About five years ago I reached the point where taking an hour out to go for a cuppa with a friend became hardly worth the effort. The harsh truth was that the children would make an unacceptable amount of mess. During these coffee visits, I would have to spend every single moment watching Daisy and Lenny. I would take Lenny with me in the event of a toilet break, and pray that Daisy didn't misuse the three minutes of my absence. I would become sick of the sound of my own voice, shouting the dreaded word 'No!' which would result in three simultaneous cries of anguish, and three pairs of hands immediately covering three pairs of sensitive ears. It was no use anyway, a couple of seconds later, whatever disruptive behaviour I had interrupted would resume. Throughout the visit, I constantly pulled my children back from pet's cages and from potted plants. From tempting television screens that were within the reach of inquisitive and often mucky little hands. From half-completed jig-saws or boxes of Lego. You name it. Most normal environments are heaving with temptations, a hundred different ways for the sensory child to create disorder. Like Thing 1 and Thing 2 from *The Cat In The Hat*, Daisy and Lenny could decimate a room within minutes, but didn't have the courtesy or the mechanical, many-armed device handy to clean the mess up afterwards.

We were terrible guests. Showing up without prior warning, I would notice a fleeting look of horror on my unwilling host's face.

In our hour of need, reaching out to people, my wild offspring and I were pushing our friends and relatives further and further away.

I must say, I haven't come across many other children with autism who cause quite so much devastation in a domestic situation as mine do. I hope that your friend's child is a little more teachable, a little tamer, and that the two of them are more easily able to slot into a variety of settings.

A couple of years ago, my sister and brother-in-law chose to install locks on their kitchen and bathroom doors. They also put locks on their three girls' bedroom doors, so that precious toys and other valuables could be quickly scooped away and stored in safety for the duration of our visits. To install these locks was relatively inexpensive, the whole operation probably cost thirty pounds in total. The process only took a couple of hours, but what it meant for us was that forever after we could drop in on them with half an hour's notice. (As I'm writing this, it has just occurred to me that they may live to regret their kindness!)

So, yes, please hide or lock things away if you fear them getting spoiled. Mum really won't be offended, she more than likely has to hide many of her own things away from her child's inquisitive little fingers. Speaking from experience, she will only be relieved to find that she is able to relax for the duration of her visit, without having to keep her eagle-eyed stare trained on her child.

As well as taking the 'locking away of valuables' stance, you can also think proactively. My Mum saves small balls of leftover wool from her knitting and crocheting projects. Both Daisy and Lenny are so enchanted by these colourful by-products of Grandma's industry that they become blind to her ornaments and her photograph frames. For a good half an hour they will dangle and tangle the little balls of wool, sometimes fighting over a particularly appealing yarn. Until the fascination wears off or the balls become so intertwined that the colourful knot cannot be shared peacefully between my youngest two children, I am free to enjoy a coffee and a chat and have a little space to catch my breath. This clever diversion costs nothing but a bit of thought, but again, it makes a short visit possible.

If you're inviting your friend and her child for lunch, take the easy route and make something very simple. This can be prepared beforehand, so that during the visit you can help to keep her little one entertained and out of mischief. I can assure you that, given the choice of a gourmet lunch or a pleasant hour with a bit of help thrown in for good measure, she will go for your company, the tinned soup and sandwich every time.

For family parties on my husband's side, we have in the past stayed with my sister-in-law. On each of these occasions she has prepared well for our arrival: her many pot plants being evacuated to the garage, the decorative coals from her electric fire are gently removed and stored somewhere out of sight. Biscuits, cereals and other irresistibles are all locked well away. These visits have still proven tricky. During the most recent, Lenny managed to flood his aunty's bathroom, behead the majority of her garden flowers and shred a full packet of toilet tissues. A hat trick! But my sister-in-law's careful preparation did make things easier for us. Her groundwork made our visit possible. Not only that, but the fact that she was prepared to go so far out of her way to make things easier for us demonstrated beyond all reasonable doubt that, despite the obvious drawbacks, she was happy to have us.

Being aware of Daisy and Lenny's love of splashing water, my sister and brother-in-law in Portsmouth once prepared for our arrival by rigging up an elaborate display with hose pipe, washing line and paddling pool. It was an excellent, captivating invention that engaged our younger two for at least an hour until their fascination was commandeered by a garden pond filled with fat, golden koi carp. I find it so touching when people go to such efforts to delight my children. If your visitor is nursing even the slightest suspicion that her presence might not be wholly appreciated, then any one of these small gestures will go a long way towards allaying her innermost fears.

If your home environment really is too cherished, too chock-full of antiques or valuables to run the risk of breakages or disruption, then please make time to visit your friend in her own home or arrange to meet on neutral territory. Her home may seem bleak as, step-by-step and year-by-year, she is forced to customise it to meet her child's needs. It may not be plush or particularly conducive to relaxation. I am sure that there are places you would rather spend your free time, but put yourself in your friend's shoes. Part by part, her world is closing down. As a result of many different factors, her liberty is being compromised. If you have ever been hospitalised for any length of time, then you know without doubt how revitalising even a short visit from a friend can be. Remember how, with every security bleep admitting callers to the ward, you felt a tingle of hope, hoping that the next visitor might be yours.

Nowadays, I have half a dozen homes that I can confidently visit with my children. I also find that it is always worth the effort. Friends and family are everything to me. I find that a quick chat with someone dear to me can be almost medicinal.

For my part, I tend to keep my visits short and clean up any spillages or sprinklages before I leave. The way I see it, it's the very least I can do.

Birthdays and Christmases used to be very tricky for me. What should I buy for my children when the only things that they seemed passionate about were packets of rice, piles of stones or huge bags of birdseed? It goes against the teachings of our increasingly materialistic society to opt out of the whole present exchange element of Christmas. A good mother buys things for her children. She scrimps and saves all year if necessary, to unveil with a flourish on the big day, the latest games console, a brand new bike, or painted dollhouse. My kids have never wanted any of this stuff. They see past the packaging, through advertising hype. They just see piles of brightly coloured plastic in boxes, good for nothing but tripping up over or crushing underfoot. In their innocence, they are astute.

Even Rosie is largely non-materialistic. By choice she buys all of her outfits from charity shops; with her no nonsense pragmatism she sees that this makes sense. She realises that she gets so much more for her money, and the money that she does spend goes to good causes. She has hours of fun customising garments, and assembling unique outfits from the vast array of previously owned clothes on her rail. She always looks fabulous!

We were in New York recently for a speaking engagement where she had been hired to motivate three hundred young people with disabilities. The contract had stated that she should dress in 'business wear.' Foolishly, I had left her to sort out her own packing, only to discover on arrival that her hand luggage boasted nothing but two pairs of ripped jeans, an assortment of men's t-shirts and some lengths of silver fabric. I was even more shocked after the presentation to find that the young people queuing to ask Rosie questions were not so much interested in the way that she had used her autism to her advantage, career-wise. No, though that was the essence of the talk that she had delivered, her fans chiefly wanted fashion advice.

For Christmas and birthdays Rosie only ever asks for books, and even then insists that I check Amazon to see if I can get them secondhand before wasting money on new copies. Even as a tiny child, she loved second hand things. To Rosie, if something had a history this did not take from its value. The fact that it had a past life before ending up in her care added something, made the item more exotic. Her unusual perspective on used goods is something that I understand and admire.

There are a great many reasons for me to feel pride in my children, and this refusal to be duped by materialism is certainly one of them. It does, however, pose a problem when people ask what to buy them for Christmas. So here are a few practical suggestions.

CDs and DVDs tend not to last very long in our household. A few plays down the line they become chewed and scratched (favourite ones taste so much better, evidently) so replacing much loved films and albums is always a good idea.

If you have a bigger budget, an outdoor trampoline will be worth its weight in gold. Daisy, late to walk and still unsteady on her feet, delights in spending many hours bouncing on the trampoline, and apart from her bi-weekly swim, this is one of her only ways to get regular exercise. I love to watch her bounce the evening away on her feet or bottom. The trampoline also serves as a giant outdoor play-pen. She can take her toys out there and play in comfort and relative safety, away from the cold or wet floor or shielded from direct sunshine by the netting.

Another great gift is a voucher for a day trip or experience. The Deep at Hull is one of our favourite destinations; we go several times each year and the children never seem to tire of the graceful motion of ghostly jellyfish or the giant spotted rays that glide along the waterbed pebbles. It's possible to purchase vouchers for family days out to zoos, farms, museums and theme parks. A cost-free but invaluable gift could also be your pledge to go along on the day trip with your friend and her little one, to lend a helping hand and help make the memories.

Cheaper options are home-made sensory boxes, filled with the kinds of small toys that I've suggested before as motivators. Balloons, marbles, light up or squeezy balls, fans, play-dough, bean-bags. Balls of string. For the very sensory child, there really is no need to break the bank, although when you are assembling sensory boxes for children who like to explore with their mouths, do check with Mum as to what is likely to go down the hatch.

More practicalities – if you are good at filling in forms, you can use this skill to make your friend's life a whole lot easier. The world of special needs is awash with paperwork. Many of the forms that your friend will be asked to fill in can take hours to complete. If she is tired or depressed then filling in intrusive, complex forms can seem like too demanding a task, hardly worth the additional financial benefits or support services that she is applying for. Your friend may need a gentle push towards making applications for extra money. It's something that many people struggle with, being given money to compensate for a child's developmental delay. In the early days, financial assistance may not seem relevant, Mum may be completely in the dark about how much in the way of extra resources that her family is going to need, and it can seem almost immoral to gain financially from this situation. Trust me, in time, all will become clear! Your friend will need all the help that she can get, both in monetary terms and through services. A few kind words of reassurance from you may be the push that she needs to get the ball rolling.

The nature of the information that she will be required to submit can serve to make mum more depressed still. The Current Disability Living Allowance (or PIP) form requires the parent or carer to go through every aspect of a child's development with a fine toothed comb, giving very specific details about any area where the child is falling behind, or needs help over and above that which the average child would require. In every other area of our parenting we are encouraged to think positively about our child's development, to celebrate successful progression and focus on the achievements that our children make.

Even this far into my journey as a special needs mum, the dreaded DLA form still fills me with despair. When the ominous brown envelope lands on my welcome mat, my heart sinks. I locate the photocopy of the last form that I filled in, copying many of the disloyal words that I wrote three years previously. Sometimes things have changed for the better in the thirty-six months since I last made the claim, and sometimes things have become more challenging. I tear through the form as quickly as I can, trying only to think practically about our difficulties and to divorce my feelings from the treacherous words that I need to write about my kids. I always feel as though I am selling them down the river. The process leaves me feeling despondent and melancholy for days afterwards. Worst case scenarios fill every page of the lengthy document, reminding me how hard my life is compared to that of the 'normal' parent.

I know that this is a big ask, and I get that you may not feel entirely confident about tackling forms on your friend's behalf, but if you know the child well and are familiar with the process of applying for funds, then to relieve your friend of the weighty burden of this task could be a wonderful thing. Of course, Mum knows the child best, and is in the best place to supply the details of what are the most challenging aspects of parenting him, but Mum is also the one who is going to be the most hurt by dwelling on these differences.

Another practical way that you can make yourself of valuable service to your friend is to be available for hospital, developmental or educational appointments. Your friend is still very raw. She is likely to become distracted or upset during these meetings.

Good professionals will be very much aware of this, and will make sure that Mum leaves the meeting with all of the information that she needs. Unfortunately, some aren't this sensitive. I came away from many of my children's early meetings realising that I hadn't asked all of the questions that I needed to, or at other times, I had asked the relevant questions, making my way steadily down my list of things to query, but not really listened to, or absorbed the answers. Often I was too busy keeping an eye on the children, or I was too tired or distracted to concentrate.

Sometimes professionals use jargon that is difficult to decipher. In those early days I often felt too silly or inexperienced to admit to any lack of knowledge. I simply nodded blankly, hoping for the best. The use of jargon in meetings to undermine parents is one of my pet hates. It's not always done intentionally, but still, that's no excuse. I have heard far too many stories of people being silenced by this sneaky treatment. Now, when professionals pipe up with the abbreviations, official talk or buzzwords, I ask them to explain straight away, to put what they are saying into layman's terms. I now find no need to be embarrassed by any lack of knowledge on my part. Sometimes this takes people aback, especially in an 'Emperor's New Clothes' situation when it transpires that the professionals themselves are not always one hundred per cent sure what a certain phrase means. Nowadays, when attending meetings, I say whatever is on my mind, with no consideration at all for what I am expected to say. I've built a lot of confidence over the years, and while they are not always enjoyable, meetings are much easier for me now. I regularly offer to support other mums through the early meetings, as I feel so strongly that there tends to be an unfair bias against the mum, who is often the only person in the room unfamiliar with the format, the jargon and the underlying reasons for calling the meeting in the first place. I also feel that it would be a crying shame to waste all of the experience that I've amassed over the years.

Turning the clock back a decade or so, I sure would have appreciated back-up from a friend like you.

Wizzarding, Stimming and Other Forms of Self Expression

'Well, he doesn't look autistic' is one of those phrases you hear repeatedly when you have one foot in the world of autism. I hear it from people in relation to Lenny, and to Rose, if you swap the 'he' for a 'she' (on the days that it is necessary to swap the pronoun – but more about this in the next chapter). I hear it from frustrated mums who feel disbelieved everywhere they go. There really is no autistic look. It does often strikes me that autistic people have a certain kind of unconscious beauty, and I think that this has something to do with the fact that they are often touchingly unaware of their good looks. Too much self-awareness of a person's own physical beauty can be quite an ugly thing, I think. But aside from this involuntary loveliness, we have to look to a person's behaviour before we are able to see any sign of the autism. In the case of high functioning autists, you would probably have to get to know them quite well before their autism became apparent.

When people meet my family for the first time, they tend to afford Daisy much more leeway, as her features, low muscle tone, wheelchair and splints make her disability instantly evident. She is never presumed naughty or spoilt, in fact the opposite is true. On occasions where she is being naughty, people tend to nod understandingly, the unspoken consensus being that she is altogether absolved of any behavioural responsibility.

No such absolution for her younger brother – it is so true that autism is an invisible condition. The more familiar we become with this condition, though, the more adept we are at spotting the associated behavioural patterns. Most autists engage in self-stimulating behaviours, more commonly known as 'stimming'. Typically, these behaviours can include flapping, bouncing, spinning, jumping and repetitive hand-movements. From person-to-person the behaviours are different, as is the length of time engaging in the self-stimulation. Triggers for these behaviours also differ from autist to autist. Before I knew what autism was, before I had ever heard the term 'stimming,' I had already become very familiar with the distinctive behaviours that Lenny and Rose displayed, either when they were very happy, excited, or when they were upset and or tense.

Richard, Rosie and I referred to Lenny's happy stimming behaviour as 'wizzarding', because to us it looked exactly like he was casting spells upon an object that he found particularly appealing. He would crouch very close to the object of his desire, his muse, let us say (although to the layman this item would probably seem quite unremarkable, the lid from a beaker, for example, or the plastic arm of a dismembered doll), he would regard his chosen talisman with a fierce intensity, his eyes ablaze with a certain mania, and his hands would perform a complex dance, fingers tense and claw-like. This this eerie incantation would be accompanied by a humming so resonant that the vibration could be felt in the flesh of my face. The 'wizzarding' could go on for some time, anything up to half an hour, and then abruptly, the spell would be broken, the muse would lose its appeal, and the wizard would go back to being just a boy.

I'd like to suggest to you now that to attempt to 'teach out' stimming behaviour is a not only a complete waste of time and energy, but the methods to eradicate it can have a deeply detrimental effect on the child, or adult, with autism. Over the decades, so many resources have been dedicated to training people with autism to look and act normal in the mistaken belief that this training will somehow remove the autism. I view anti-stimming tuition in the same light as the practice of striking the hand of someone who holds a pen or pencil in their left hand. In fact, scrap that. I see it as a far more deeply undermining form of cruelty.

Even if a person is trained by punishment or reward to appear neurotypical, the appearance can only ever be skin deep, of that I am sure. It can never be more than an act. Inside, the person with autism is still reacting to whatever has triggered the intense response whether he has learned to contain his excitement or not. He is, and always will be, autistic.

Our best parenting advice advocates valuing children as individuals, encouraging them to express their uniqueness and originality. In striving to be the most supportive and encouraging parents that we can, we balance what we think is important for the child with what lights up and motivates them. We work with our children's natural strengths and interests. In short, we let them know that it is fine for them to be their truest selves. In the process of demonstrating that we accept them completely just as they are, we give our children the confidence to take their truest nature out into the wider world, and so we help to support the deep-rooted confidence that is essential for any person to be their best self, to live the fullest life possible. Who wouldn't want this for their child? For our society as a whole, we benefit from the vibrancy of variety, we are able to enjoy multi-coloured metropolitan glory.

Understanding the importance of being true to ourselves, and encouraging those around us to be true to themselves is the key to accepting and learning to value stimming behaviour. If, from a very young age, a child is denied the right to be who he truly is, to express himself in the ways that come naturally to him, the message is loud and clear. His parents do not accept the raw essence of his nature, and if he carries on acting in this way, the rest of the world will not accept him either. There is something amiss, something distasteful which needs to be knocked down and rebuilt, if people out there are ever going to admit him into their inner circle. I personally can imagine no more damaging a lesson, no way to more completely strip a developing child of his confidence than to demonstrate such a basic lack of belief in his core personality.

I'm telling you this partly in the hope that you will pass this observation on to your friend, should a conversation about stimming behaviours arise. I also hope that you can learn to appreciate, and even to love, the stimming behaviour of the little autist in your life.

Your friend will undoubtedly have many concerns around the extent to which her child will be accepted, how he will 'fit in.' These concerns can manifest as an irritation with the type of behaviours that she feels will single him out. Possibly, she may feel that when he engages in stimming, his autism is laid bare for all to see.

I fully understand that, from the point of view of many parents, because stimming is the only 'at-glance' difference between their child and the next, it could be tempting to fall into the trap of blaming the stimming behaviours for the child's difference. Dare I suggest that this is a topsy-turvy assumption. Stimming behaviour doesn't make a child have autism; he has autism therefore he stims. I believe that self-stimulating behaviours are a type of deep communication, as well as being a way of processing the intense surges of energy created by an off-kilter sensory and nervous system.

So if your friend were to say to you, for example, 'Look, Tommy's doing that thing again. That flapping thing. I hate it; it makes him look weird!' and you were to reply with something like, 'It's a kind of dance, I guess. You could see it as something beautiful. It's part of who he is,' then your helpful point of view could go a long way to allaying her fears, and allowing her to see the behaviour as a beneficial form of communication. Not that I would dream of putting words into your mouth.

Let's stick with Lenny for the purpose of illustration. He is a boy with very few words at his disposal. We do get to hear his voice, nowadays (a wonderful, much longed for gift!) but the language that he uses is largely echolalic, that is to say, his words are borrowed and repeated. His limited repertoire consists of lines from Disney movies, TV theme tunes, advertisement jingles, nursery rhymes and other phrases which he seems to absorb directly from his environment. The more often that phrases are repeated in his presence, the more likely he is to incorporate them into

96

his unique language of recurring echoes. The phrases that he uses give us a direct insight into the kind of things that people say to him (or in front of him) when we aren't present. His chosen words also give staff at his school and respite resources a direct spyhole into our lives, so we have to be careful! We often hear him repeat phrases like 'Lenny King, come and sit down right now!' A scribbled line in his home school book recently informed us that he has started saying 'For Christ's sake!' at school. I humbly accepted the blame for that one.

So without the gift of spontaneous language, Lenny must find a way to tell us what he wants, and to tell us how he feels about the decisions that we make on his behalf. He actually does this to great effect. It's amazing what you can cobble together with limited tools when you are desperate. Once, during a long, drawn out lecture from his dad in which Lenny was being reprimanded for sprinkling a litre carton of rice around the kitchen, he placed his hands over his ears, screwed up his face and shouted 'Father Duck says quack, quack, quack!' An ingenious use of nursery rhyme language, wouldn't you agree?

At fourteen years, he has now become quite adept at using objects from his environment to illustrate his needs. Although Lenny seems quite disinterested in the formal system of symbols that is used in his school, and which we periodically try to bring in at home, he has learned to use the real, three dimensional things that are around him to more directly communicate his wishes.

He brings his shoes or a coat if he wants to go out, making sure that I am looking in his direction before putting on a show of half-hearted adorning of clothes (back to front, inside out, wrong feet, he really doesn't have the patience for foppishly fussy dressing habits). He carefully wraps my hands around my car keys, or hangs various handbags from my shoulder like a game of real-life Buckaroo, if I have studiously ignored his haphazard donning of coat and shoes. He frequently directs our guests towards the front door when he grows weary of their visit (always an awkward turn of events). He brings an assortment of bikinis, swimming trunks and a towels should he decide that we are all in need of some exercise. So on and so forth. His symbols are the things that are to hand, the things that he can grab and thrust towards us. Through this relatively clumsy communication technique, his basic, practical needs are usually quite easily made clear.

Much more difficult to ascertain are his more abstract aspirations. The desire to communicate affection, dreams for the future, intangible fears or other fleeting concepts is part of what it is to be human, and non-verbal autists certainly do have these desires. Lenny uses facial expression and body language when he wants to communicate his feelings and entreaties. He often gives me a kiss, or presents his forehead that I might kiss him, but if I am honest, this can be more accurately translated as a desire for a biscuit than any genuine show of affection (selfishly, I always insist on a kiss before the handing over of a biscuit. This may seem bit cruel, or in any case contractual, but I'm a mum, my only wages are kisses and hugs, and by hook or by crook I'm going to make sure that I don't work for free.)

Clumsy communication devices aside, our best clues to the way that Lenny is feeling generally, though, are the unconscious, self-stimulating behaviours that seem to happen of their own accord. The very natural, graceful dance of his stimming seems to me so much more organic than his learned, unsophisticated attempts to convey meaning. In exactly the same way that we pick up on a neurotypical person's truest mood via subliminal assessment of posture, gait, by how close they sit to us or how long they hold our gaze, the subconscious body movements of a person with autism offer the most dependable mood gauge.

We have become fondly familiar with Lenny's happy movements, his excited tip-toe dances, his hand-flapping, his resonant humming and 'wizzarding.'

Lenny's happy noises, though often delivered at an intense volume, make my heart sing with gladness. I see his 'wizzarding' as a living applause, a physical appreciation of whatever it is that engages him, draws him into our world.

Of course, not all stimming is a result of this intense happiness. Some behaviours represent internal stress or anxiety. And we are all too familiar with Lenny's stress-stims. We see him biting down on the heels of his hands, which have become irreparably calloused over the years. When he is unsure of something, we see Lenny stepping back and forth, back and forth over the invisible thresholds between rooms, as though to commit to being in one room or the other would be far too great a gamble. For people with autism, stress often leaks out, and can be seen in the form of rocking or head-banging.

However unpleasant it is for us as carers to witness this painful display, we must not discourage it; we must recognise it as the highly effective communication that it is. To punish, ban or 'teach out' self-stimulating behaviour is to deny the non-verbal child his voice. For someone who has no words, or who's words can't be fully relied upon to express their true feelings, stimming can also be a very useful outlet for tension. For the attending parent or carer, it can be a vital indication as to what is going on in the child's psyche.

Even for the most adept of communicators amongst us, we know that the masking of our innermost feelings is detrimental – a short-cut to breakdown. When our autistic loved ones are engaged in stimming behaviours, I believe that they are showing us their most sincere selves, and that this should never be denied.

Here's another angle to consider when deliberating the necessity of stimming, or ritualised behaviours. When we look back through history, the less that our ancestors actually knew about their environment, the less control that they had over their lives and their futures, the more heavily they relied on ritual, tradition and superstition. This ritualistic behaviour of our ancestors can be interpreted as a desperate attempt to control outcomes with respect to unpredictable events that directly affected their lives, for example, the climate, the success of a harvest, or the spreading of infectious disease. As our knowledge of science grew, our reliance on ritual and ceremony became less necessary.

When we put ourselves in the shoes of a non-verbal autist, it very quickly becomes apparent that the world is a most unpredictable, volatile environment. Inexplicable changes happen all of the time. Without the benefit of explanation, or explanation's indispensable partner, understanding, we see that the landscape of an autist's life is capricious and unstable. The terror of this unpredictability can be lessened somewhat with the aid of visual timetables and other communication aids, but even these cannot always be trusted. Sudden change happens, bringing doubt and apprehension in its wake. With limited communication skills, impaired understanding, lack of theory of mind, who can blame the autist for reverting to the comfort of ritualised behaviour, if it is the only defence mechanism available?

Stimming is not a behaviour that is limited to non-verbal autists. The are many autists who need less support and who are able to fit in, behave 'normally' with normal body movements, socially acceptable behaviour. Many of these people may be able to maintain the charade for the duration of a university lecture, a morning at the office or a full school day. Once back to the safety and comfort of their home environment, though, stimming behaviours can be a longed for indulgence. Stimming is perhaps a de-stressing method through which the autist is able to become calm and be true to his own nature.

When Rosie is stimming (or imagining, as she insists on it being called), she trots around and around in a circle. She has done this ever since she was tiny. We found it unbearably cute when she was a toddler. It was as though the circular path that she followed led her to another world, a dimension that was clearly far more engaging than the drab, everyday world that she shared with us. Her hands would flap and dance, a little skip and a jump here and there might interrupt her well-worn path. Odd, one-sided snippets of conversation would shoot from her mouth, crossing the void from her imagined dimension, giving us a taste of what adventures she might be living out.

'Rosie rescued the kitten!'

'Look at Rosie, I never knew she could do that!'

'The mountains are moving!'

'She can hear what the animals are thinking!'

It was always quite clear from these disjointed sentences that in her other world, Rosie was some kind of a hero, or God. Even if it had been within my power to do so, how could I ever have wrenched her from this mystical kingdom whose citizens held her in such high regard? I never considered calling her back, or telling her to stop for fear of her being considered 'weird' or different. As far as I was concerned, any friends who couldn't accept this display of her beautiful soul did not deserve her friendship. She still occasionally treads the circular path that leads directly to her magical domain, and to be perfectly honest, I feel quite envious. Sometimes I wish the doorway to the magical kingdom that she can visit was open to me.

Daisy's 'wizzarding' is closer to regular dancing than the typical stimming behaviour that would normally be recognised in someone with autism. Like her big sister, Daisy tends to go around and around in circles when she is at her happiest. Hers is a celebration dance that brings a smile to the face of anyone lucky enough to be watching. With or without music to accompany her movement, she throws back her head of golden curls, aiming smiles to the ceiling or sky, and waves her arms in the air. Daisy is unsteady on her feet at the best of times, so this flailing around of her arms and upper body often results in a rather ungainly fall. Fortunately, the padding of her nappy prevents bottom-bruises. She soon puts the indignity behind her, climbs to her feet and resumes her blissful pirouetting.

Now that he is older, Lenny's stimming has changed in nature. Only rarely do we glimpse the 'wizard boy' of old.

It's difficult to tell whether he has copied Rosie's style of self-stimulation or whether his own behaviour has simply evolved. When he is content though, you will nowadays find him walking or skipping round and around in a circle. Sometimes Rosie and Lenny do this together, in opposite directions, the circumferences of their own private circles crossing over because of the compact nature of our living room. Each sibling seems oblivious to the other, until they collide mid living-circuit.

When we think logically about it, stimming behaviour is in no way restricted to those on the spectrum. Imagine the most stressful of situations (you're stuck in traffic on the motor-way, on the way to the airport, you didn't leave quite enough time to account for delays and you are in real danger of missing your plane). What kind of behaviours would you notice slipping through the veneer of your calm exterior? Hand-biting? Toe-tapping? Stressed humming, or repeated swearing? Meaningless, repeated phrases like 'come on come on come on,' even though nobody is there to hear or to act on your words? None of these behaviours make any sense, nor are they all that far removed from the stress stims that we observe in the behaviour of people with autism.

And what about when we are at our happiest, or most excited? Imagine discovering that you've won a large amount of money on the national lottery. Millions! Could you keep your body still, at the prospect of spending all of that lovely money? Would you skip and dance, might you jump up and down, or repeat phrases over and over? 'Oh my God, oh my God, oh my God!'

Here's something that I consider to be an invaluable and illuminative window. Because of the uncommon nature of my family, I have come to recognise that the autists among us who do have the gift of words are the people who are best able to shed clarifying light on the behaviours of those who don't. Before even attempting to write this chapter, I asked Rosie for her take on stimming behaviour. I asked her to sum it up as briefly as she could, why did she do it? What benefits were there to stimming? What would it mean to her if, for some reason, she was not allowed to stim or to 'imagine?' The simple answer that she gave only serves to back up my resolution to never, ever interfere, and to leave stimming behaviours well alone.

She said, 'Stimming is like breathing. You might die if you didn't do it.'

I like to call this one 'The reluctant vampire'

Daisy in her mainstream setting – Sports day with me and her beloved Miss Parker.

Cooling down on a July afternoon

Happy days out and about

Lenny at twelve months – already an accomplished climber

Caravan holiday 2004, the happiest of times

Keeping the bingo wings at bay

Lenny aged 18 months exploring his environment.

Lenny and Rose join Daisy in bed for cuddles

Sisterly love, 2003

Daisy on the beach 2012 – keeping clean is not an option

Rosie aged 2 and Daisy 6 months

Daisy with her Grandad on her first birthday

Dinner by the cat-flap

Daisy and Lenny at their most content

Growing up – Daddy's boy

Girls Photo-shoot

Lenny at 14, handsome despite home-cut hair

Deeper Wisdom

For as far back as history is documented, those among us with learning disabilities have suffered at the hands of our harsh judgement and our lack of understanding. Though the kindest, best organised of our societies have offered pity, charity and a little compassion, a brief flick through the narrative of our past treatment of the differently abled does not make for comfortable reading.

And yet, the more I read and learn about deeper wisdom, the more I see this real, direct understanding of reality in my children, and in the other learning disabled people that I am lucky enough to get to know.

Eckharte Tolle invites us to treasure the present, sure as he is that this is all that can ever truly exist. He asks that we open our senses to all that is, all that we can perceive at this very moment in time. The past is nothing but a swirling mass of lingering memories, shifting shape according to our mood. When we yearn to experience fond nostalgia, the kaleidoscope of our memory shifts to present the visions that best evoke this feeling. When our passions are aroused, and we long for the version of events that best justifies our resentment, we twist to justify our antagonism, and lo and behold, there before us the ghost of some past injustice returns to haunt us. When we begin to understand that there is nothing but this fleeting present moment, that all that lies behind and ahead of us is as insubstantial and unreliable as smoke, then at last we can become free of fear, free of resentment, and free of the echoes of pain that can haunt the present and cast the shadow of gloom over our future.

Although Daisy and Lenny may lack the communication skills to debate the merits of mindfulness, I am reminded every day that this is their habitual practice.

While he is in his preferred, natural environment, every atom of Lenny's being is attuned to the beauty around him. Running water reflects dazzling glimmers of sunlight that are more spectacular than any man-made firework display. The captivating show caused by the frantic orange sparks of a bonfire; delicate dandelion seeds floating languorously on a gentle summer breeze; these are the invaluable treasures that nature offers to him. They are treasures that cost nothing, that no amount of money could ever buy, that can never be owned or stolen. He need waste none of his time or energy collecting or guarding these treasures that delight him so, because each and every day he is offered more of the same. Every moment presents new fascination for the boy who knows where to look. Even indoors, the trickle of water delights, a shard of light illuminates the myriad world of floating dust-motes, shredded tissue thrown to the air becomes half a dozen tiny parachutes, sashaying to defy the pull of gravity that eventually claims them.

From Lenny's perspective, the world is a fascinating dimension filled with indescribable beauty. Each moment delivers more wonderful gifts for him to behold.

Daisy occupies that magical place in time that is the ever present now. She never laments past events and never fears what the future will bring. There have been times when she has been horribly ill, sickly and poisoned from within by an infected appendix, struggling for every ragged breath as both of her lungs became spongy with the wet rot of pneumonia. When these illnesses miraculously passed, did Daisy languish in her sick bed, eking out the sympathy value or raking over the sadness of her misfortune? Of course not! She rejoiced in the fact that she was well again. I still recall, after a lengthy and miserable hospital stay, taking her out for some fresh air on a summer's afternoon. We walked through a vibrant field of yellow dandelions, a thousand merry suns swaying beneath the china blue sky. She swished at the long, overgrown weeds, cannula still burrowed into the back of her tiny, fragile hand. She threw back her head and laughed for the sheer joy of being free from the hospital bed, and being able to witness the blinding glory of nature.

Rosie frequently pulls the shard of truth from a situation. I try to weigh problems up, changing stance to see a situation from the angle of each person involved. It's exhausting, and soon becomes far too complex. I become bogged down with the different layers of reasoning, and end up chasing my thought processes like a dog trying to catch its own tail. Not so my daughter. Her simple, matter-of-fact TED talk gained her a standing ovation at the Kennedy Center in Washington DC. The conference was awash with academics, professors and seasoned public speakers. It was Rosie's first ever public speech and she had composed it in her bedroom six weeks prior to the event.

The audience (me and her father included) were absolutely blown away by the simple, gleaming truth of her observations. She reminded us that we are all fascinating individuals. She asked us, why hide the beautiful light that we are behind the bland camouflage of convention. Why not allow one another to be spectacular, original and unique?

It's my humble opinion that we would all do well to put aside the part of ourselves that longs to teach, to lecture and to be praised for our wisdom. Our children, our young people and our learning disabled brothers and sisters have much to teach us, if only we are able to let go of the illusory notion of ourselves as mere instructors.

Only yesterday I met a young autistic savant who was able to perform amazing mental feats of calculation. Alex's proud mum checked his mental arithmetic on her calculator and showed me how accurate he was. I have heard many stories of autists with such amazing abilities, and I was deeply impressed. His knack with sums was not the thing that amazed me most about Alex, however. For each member of his family, each friend, and each new person that he met, he attributed a colour, and a surprising description. After regarding me solemnly for a few moments, he told me that I was a Light Blue Astronaut, and Rosie a Silver Flyer. His verbal communication is still at an early stage, so I was unable to prise from him the reckoning behind these fascinating descriptions. I acutely felt that he had much to teach me, though, and that there was much more than randomness to these carefully thought out metaphors.

Experience has taught me that when I meet a person with autism I must become deferential, humble. I must drop any preconceptions, and open my senses to them in exactly the way that Lenny makes himself open to the natural world. This way, I am best able to learn, and to see the beauty that is before me.

Boys and Girls

Statistically speaking, at the time of writing, my intended reader is far more likely to be applying my theories, philosophies and advice to the little boy autist in her life than the little girl. Glancing back over the completed chapters, I have repeatedly referred to 'he' when talking about your friend's child, and this is no coincidence. In early 2016, the latest figures show that the ratio of boys to girls receiving a diagnosis of autism is 4:1. Go back ten years or so and this ratio would be much steeper, something like 9:1. That's as precise as I am prepared to get with facts and figures, for fear of making some libellous error and getting myself into trouble. By the time this book is finished and published, the stats will have changed anyway, working their way towards that perfect equilibrium, the 50:50 mark that I believe to be truly representative.

There is no grammatically smooth pronoun to describe both or either sexes. 'They' sounds horribly clumsy, especially when we are referring to a single person. 'He/she' doesn't exactly trip off the tongue. 'It' is downright rude. My feeling, though, is that before much longer, we are going to have to invent a pronoun that is much more ambiguous, and we're going to have to start getting used to working this word into our spoken and written language. May I add that this grammatical evolution will not be purely for the benefit of pedantic writers who tire of specifying that when they say 'he' they might just as easily mean 'she.'

In the past autism has been described as a male disorder, or even 'extreme maleness.' More recently, though, understanding has grown to the realisation that there are also a great number of girls with autism, and that their condition can affect them in very different ways from their male counterparts. We are slowly beginning to realise that female autistic traits can be very different from the historically accepted picture of Vulcan-like logical thinking or trainspotting nerdiness that popular culture would sign off as the neatly wrapped up package – autism for beginners.

We are well aware that autism offers 'peaks of ability' which sometimes soar to the dizzy heights of savantism. Often the talents of girls centre around social mimicry. We see chameleons, adept at adaptation, highly skilled when it comes to absorbing the mannerisms of those in the social circle perceived to be winning the popularity game.

Acting, though, can be exhausting. After just a couple of scenes most actors tend to need a break, a drink with the understudy, or an hour in the dressing room away from the spotlights.

My own experience tells me that acting for any length of time can lead to the undoing of the actor or actress.

I have come this far with no diagnosis, but recognise many of these recently recognised 'female autism' traits in my character. Looking back to the early days of my childhood, these character traits seem much more exaggerated, much more obvious. Being motivated to pinpoint these traits in my younger self, I appreciate, may be partly due to my absolute immersion in the subject of autism. I've become a bit obsessed with it, and spot autistic attributes in many of the people that I know.

I was a strange child though. Often gloomy, I was absolutely obsessed with mortality. In the 1970s, talk of nuclear war was all about. It seemed to be a foregone conclusion that the atom bomb would neatly eradicate the whole of humanity. Regular public service announcements beamed out advice, recommending certain courses of action that might be taken to provide the best chance of survival; unscrewing an internal door, leaning it against a sturdy wall, padding it with sandbags to provide a tiny, triangular sanctuary in which to live through the apocalypse. I completely obsessed over this propaganda. I jumped from detailed survival plan to prayers for a quick end to it all, to save humanity from the horrors of the aftermath. Thoughts of my own death, and the death of my family and friends, were never far from my mind.

I could easily conceal my melancholy persona, though. Sometimes, If I needed to, I would become the class clown. It wasn't at all difficult for me to make people laugh. For most of the time, I loved this role, but at other times I fiercely resented the pressure that I felt under to amuse people. And then on another day, I would feel an overwhelming compulsion to rebel against any authority, encouraging classroom anarchy, winning no friends amongst teaching staff.

Academically I was able, but unless the subject being taught was one of my special interests, I was bored and completely disengaged. I was quirky, and felt inwardly different from even the closest of my friends. It was easy for me to get 'in with the in crowd' – sometimes I did, but other times I preferred to stay on the edge of things. I often wondered if the people around me genuinely liked me, or if they were just drawn to the character that I was playing at any given time. Things came to a head when I was eleven years old. I distinctly remember plotting to 'fall-out' with everyone who hung around with me so that I could lead a blissful, friendless life doing whatever the hell I might choose – reading, collecting, writing stories and practicing my flute during school break-times. Although an outside observer might have considered that I had been popular, I deeply felt that my popularity was undeserved and even unwanted. You can only pretend for so long.

At the time I considered that this unfriending of my friends to be something of a social breakthrough. At last I had the time and the peace and quiet that I felt I needed to develop my own interests. I have always been a lucid dreamer (alert and conscious within the setting of my dreams and sometimes able to manipulate events within the dream) and sleeping/dreaming was one of my all-time favourite hobbies. I would sneak to my room after school, on the pretence of doing homework or reading. Instead I would draw the curtains, tuck myself in and will myself to sleep in order to experience the vibrant, exclusive adventures that were always playing out in my subconscious. These adventures invariably involved me flying 'Superman' style over beautiful landscapes or oceans. It was the realisation that I was flying that alerted me to the fact that I was here at last, in the beautiful dream world, where the laws of gravity didn't seem to apply.

Of course, my eleven-year-old self didn't see what all the fuss was about, but my mother became very concerned about my sudden friendlessness and the subsequent retreat into my bedroom and my internal world. She took me first to the doctor, who prescribed a tonic wine of which I was to imbibe one glass before bedtime (looking back, I cannot help but to question the wisdom of this alcohol therapy, but at the time I thought it was bloody brilliant). My next appointment was with a middle-aged lady who constantly encouraged me to draw illustrations of my dreams, and while drawing talk about how I felt in certain situations (A therapist! With time, all becomes clear!) I am fairly sure that in a similar case nowadays the autism question would be raised, but at the time it was neatly concluded that I had an aversion to school life and would grow out of my reclusive behaviour with time.

In a way, the lady with the crayons was right. As the years went by, I learned to compensate for my quirkiness, mended friendships and made new acquaintances. My dreaming world was still a large part of my life, but I became savvy enough to work out who to talk to about the 'waking dreams' and when to keep the information to myself. As I progressed to my teenage years and learning became much more subject specific, I rediscovered academic joy in art and literature.

In the eyes of the world, I became 'normal' again.

My pre-teen social crash (albeit more of a kamikaze style crash than an accidental one) is of particular interest to me, because recently I have seen it happen time and time again to a certain type of young girl in our social circle. Rosie, right on cue aged eleven, promptly disengaged from her friends and her studies and withdrew to her own internal world. I can think of at least half a dozen other young girls who have spontaneously abandoned their friendships, and have instead chosen a period of social isolation.

These days, soon after the therapist or counsellor is engaged, the girls are invariably flagged up for an autism assessment. It seems quite obvious to me that the crash happens at this age to very sensitive young girls because this is exactly the point at which the social sphere becomes mind-bogglingly complex. Less sensitive children might be blissfully unaware of the many layers of complexity involved in every social interaction. They will happily continue to plough through their chosen path within the social sphere, and will be much less likely to retreat to an uncomplicated, controllable inner world.

The crash seems even more likely to happen in the cases of girls who have slipped through the diagnosis net, but, like the ten-year-old me, have many suppressed autistic traits. These children are largely unsupported, being left to sink or swim in the complicated social arena of school life. One of the most noticeable differences these days is that the crash is often accompanied by a sudden loss of appetite or some other form of eating disorder, self-harming behaviours, sexual identity and orientation issues, followed by medical and counselling appointments and, ultimately, medication.

Another point worthy of consideration is that girls have a natural leaning towards effective communication. In short, we love to chat. Typically, male communication is all about the practical exchange of information, even in a social setting (please excuse the generalisation). In groups of young boys we see a lot of physical behaviour, shouting, pushing, and competitive displays of physical skills. Observe a typical group of men talking and you might notice each taking turns at being centre-stage, telling a well-worn story, an anecdote, or passing on some nugget of wisdom, while the rest of the group encourages, heckles and cheers. I have joked in the past that talking 'with' my husband is sometimes like being pelted with information bullets; they are fired in my direction with little or no encouragement. I am a target for his conversational munitions, rather than an active participant. Conversations with my female friends are much gentler, and we tend to court and offer opinions subtly. There is invariably at least as much listening as talking going on. Essentially, like the ability to socially 'blend-in,' the natural communication skills of girls and women alike can make for a misleading cover-up.

OK, hands up, confession time. I am very conscious of the fact that, in the last few paragraphs, I have somewhat gracelessly cleaved the whole of the humanity into male and female camps. Gentle, inquisitive communicators vs testosterone driven war-mongers (not that I am biased!) How dull our world would be if things were that simple. With my growing understanding of the subtler gender delineations, especially in those who have autism, I really ought to know better.

I am one hundred per cent sure that there is a connection between androgyny and autism. Of course, this does not mean that I think that every autist is androgynous, but amongst those that I know and meet, I see a general trend that is impossible to ignore. Whether this is something intrinsically linked to the autistic biology and character, or whether autists are just more inclined to be true to themselves, less likely to mindlessly bleat and follow the crowd of sheep, I am not qualified to say. Perhaps it is time for a scientific study to clarify the connection, or perhaps it is better to simply accept and appreciate the fact that our autistic siblings do not necessarily fit so neatly into one or other of the gender delineations.

Even before the event of our birth, our society delights in squishing and coercing us into the socially acceptable form of 'boy' or 'girl' and later, of 'man' or 'woman.' Expecting a baby boy? Paint his room powder blue with an unsubtle theme of cars, trains or dynamic superheroes. Maybe opt for a theme of planets and space exploration, if you are more ambitious about his prospective career? A little girl? Great, adorn the pastel room with excessive frills, hang pictures of fairies, kick start her collection of baby dolls to prepare her for a lifetime of nurturing and femininity!

Rosie was never that easy to pin down. She rejected the teddy bears and dolls that she was given as a small child in favour of a bug-eyed silver alien called 'Zed' and a plastic dog on wheels, which she pedantically christened 'Vehicle-Dog'.

At almost eighteen, she now defines herself as 'gender fluid nonbinary'.

From a very young age Rosie would spend weeks on end dressing, and acting, as a boy. These masculine periods were interspaced with other character dress-up phases, such as a Victorian maid, a spikey haired punk princess and a home-spun superhero called 'Doctor Dare'. Doctor Dare's sidekick was a female cat, who went by the name of 'Nurse Kitty.' The part of this feline assistant was played by Lenny, although as far as I could tell, he was completely unaware of his role in the ongoing super-heroic drama.

When Rosie first began to take clothes from her little brother's wardrobe I assumed it was connected with the fact that she was extremely sensitive to the texture of fabrics, and found boys' clothes more comfortable than girls'. She was only around seven years old at the time, and, even though Lenny was big for his age, she struggled to squeeze her limbs into the soft fabric of his jogging bottoms and hoodies. She even preferred his underpants to the stuff in her own underwear draw.

I attempted to address the situation, and took her along on shopping trips, so that she could make her own choices from the garments in the girls' department, testing the clothes for softness of fabric as we went along. As I selected various dresses and skirts for her perusal, though, she would pull a disgusted face, and sidle over to the boys' department.

This learning towards androgyny wasn't too much of a worry for us, in the grand scheme of things. Richard and I were always very happy with our little tomboy. Anyway, I had the very girly, completely compliant Daisy. She was content to let me dress her up in ribbons and frills, and, with her cascade of golden curls, always looked the picture of femininity.

I think Rosie was eight years old when she had her first alarmingly boyish haircut. I remember waiting in the local hairdressers with her, until it was time for her to take her place at the hair-washing basin. Daisy and Lenny were growing restless in their huge side-by-side buggy, starting to grab and irritate one-another. Also, I needed a few items of shopping, so, promising Rosie that I'd be back in twenty minutes, I told her that she was in charge and that she could let the hairdresser know exactly how she wanted her hair.

What I had imagined was that she might like the responsibility of deciding whether or not to opt for a fringe, whether to stick with her long plaits or go for a more fashionable bob. I returned with my carrier full of groceries hung on the handlebars of Daisy and Lenny's buggy to find that Rosie had instructed the young hairdresser to give her an all over number three cut, with an inch or so of spikey, gelled fringe. Quite a trim! The horrified look must have been evident on my face, as the young girl with the scissors told me 'Rosie said she had agreed this style with you, is it OK?'

In time, I found that it was OK. I found that Rosie's determination to dress as a boy wasn't the only unusual development in our family's chosen fashion expression.

Ever sensitive to the assaults of nail scissors and hair trimmers, Lenny grew beautifully long talons and opted to wear his soft, sandy hair at shoulder length. To us he only ever looked gorgeous, cutting a muscular, Tarzan-like figure in his wildness. All would have been well, but we were often faced with notes in his school or respite book asking us to give his nails a 'quick trim.'.This two-word instruction was far easier to carry out in theory than it was in reality. The only way I could comply (without setting off the mother-of-all-meltdowns) was to cut Lenny's fingernails and hair while he was sleeping. As I am sure you can appreciate, it proved rather difficult to execute this midnight grooming routine with any skill or precision. Lenny's look quickly evolved from native lupine barbarian to home-styled, raggedy-haired geek. On top of that, he was a light sleeper at the best of times, and the threat of awakening to discover a determined, scissor-wielding mother floating like a demented apparition above him seemed, if anything, to contribute to him resisting the sleep process.

Every so often, in acquiescence to the majority judgement, I would brutally shave him like a sheep, as short as possible, in order that I wouldn't have to visit this indignity on him for another six months or so. Whenever I was stronger than him, this brutal and unsettling approached worked. He hated it though, and would shake violently throughout the shearing process. Afterwards, I would reward him with a Cornetto, and it seemed that once the ice-cream was in hand my son was more than willing to forgive and forget.

By the time Lenny was nine years old, he was stronger than me. The barbaric sheep shearing business became a no-go. Gently, coaxingly, I would do my utmost to persuade him. I would mime the process of the clippers gliding over the top of his head. I would allow him to hold the clippers, with my hand over the top, to help him to feel more in control of the procedure. By this stage he could count to ten (though I am still not convinced that he understands the significance of the counting words). 'Just ten, Lenny,' I would promise him. Then, as I carefully stroked the cutters over his scalp, I would count 'One, Two, Three, Four...' always stopping at 'Ten'. This way, I hoped to gain his trust, and let him know that the torture would not go on forever. It worked fairly well, although, at that rate, a haircut could take weeks. Because his hair was long prior to the extreme cut, strands would pull and snag. Although Lenny is generally hardy and has a high pain threshold, he found this particular torture unbearable, and the whole thing became a bit of a nightmare.

On one memorable occasion, I managed to shave the crown of Lenny's head down to a fairly even 'number two' stubble, with the fringe, sides and back of his hair still long and flowing. At this stage of the game he bolted, shaking and desperate, up to his roost on top of the television in our living room where he remained for a number of hours, singing "Bob the Builder" at a fast, highly stressed tempo. Eventually, we managed to convey a promise to leave his hair well alone. His 'monkish' look was made all the more convincing by the fact that he had, at the time, taken to wearing a grey cashmere jumper of mine. The jumper was belted at the waist, hung mid-calf length on Lenny, and was accessorised by nothing more than a pair of his dad's summer sandals. If we had a reputation as being a slightly strange family, our children's chosen takes on fashion were doing nothing to dispel this rumour.

Over the years, Lenny's relationship with clothes has proved to be an 'all or nothing' affair. As a baby, toddler, and young boy, he much preferred to go naked. Again, I was very relaxed about this, insisting only that he wore a pair of pants around the house. Grudgingly, he complied with my basic request, until all at once he decided that semi-nakedness was no longer 'en vogue'. From this point on, he piled on as many clothes as possible. He squeezed himself into t-shirt over t-shirt over t-shirt. Sometimes he would put on a jumper and then a few more t-shirts over the top of that. Once, we counted nine different t-shirts. He dressed in a speedy, comedy way, as though desperate to wear as much as possible. His bottom half remained the same, only a meagre pair of pants to cover his modesty, but his torso was bulkily clad with this system of layers, ironically with an 'Incredible Hulk' t-shirt being the final layer.

Shoes were always difficult for Lenny. In the summer, he would be happy to wear sandals for school but seemed to find any other footwear far too restrictive. He would completely refuse to wear anything at all on his feet until the very last moment, when he was due to walk out the door. How I would dread the early morning knock, when Jayne, his escort came to collect him. Here the great shoe debate would begin again. I set the options out two by two before my Lord, that he may deign to select an acceptable pair. We would often have seven or eight pairs lined up for him (I realise now that in this case too much choice was probably no choice at all; I was completely overwhelming him, and this only added to his confusion and his inability to make a choice. In my defence, my reasoning was simple – out of all these pairs, there must be one that he would find acceptable!)

Invariable, he would settle on the most ragged pair possible, if there were holes in the sole, that didn't bother Lenny. If the laces were frayed and unthreadable, who cared? As he left, holding Jayne's hand, I would implore her to reassure the school staff that he did have suitable footwear and that we weren't neglecting him.

With time and experience, I have relaxed completely about the way that my children choose to dress, and to present themselves to the world. Again and again I find, as I tread the curious path of autism parenting, that as soon as I relax completely about a certain issue, then, magically, the charge of tension that surrounded whatever our problem was falls away, like the collapse of an invisible force-field. When I no longer invest so desperately in the solution to a particular problem, then the problem seems to right itself of its own accord.

There have been some tough times over the last eighteen years. Both Lenny and Rosie have completely broken down in the past, refusing to leave the house for days on end, leaving me unable to imagine what kind of future we might experience, as individuals and as a family. On three separate occasions, Daisy's health has deteriorated to the point where hospital staff refused to be prompted into reassuring me that she would recover at all. While deeply frightening, these types of experiences do serve to put things into perspective.

So what if my children are not completely feminine or not completely masculine? It's fine by me. In fact, on reflection, I have concluded that many people subconsciously invent personalities for their children, and the structure of these devised personas is commonly built around a masculine or feminine core. The parents, and eventually the children themselves, come to accept this hastily assembled character as the true essence of their nature. Because my children have always effortlessly shrugged off the mantle of this oppressive design, I have been allowed to get to know the real 'them.' The subtle, multi-dimensional truth of their reality has amazed and humbled me. So, for this gift, I am sincerely thankful.

How the children dress really means nothing to me, and it often means everything to them. In today's image conscious society, having clean, neatly presented, fashionably acceptable children means so much to so many people. If you take anything from my story, from my description of my very individual children, please take this. Let them be, if they are happy, and harming no-one in the process. Whatever they are, just let them be.

Dinner Time Tensions

Look as far back in time as you care to, or look far afield to different cultures around the globe, and it quickly becomes apparent that women have always been judged by their ability to prepare, serve and host a successful meal. By their ability to maintain their family's excellent health, and to tease their guest's appetites with skilfully prepared food. As the very good friend of an autism mum, I know that you are not judging. Your heart may be breaking for her as her culinary endeavours meet her child's needs but do not go anywhere near to satisfying his wants. You may be as worried as she is about the selective eating habits of her little autist, and you may be at a loss as to what advice to offer.

Feeding and sleeping. These two issues constantly vie for top slot on the autism mum's list of things that drive her to distraction. From the very earliest days of childhood, we spend our days fixating on how much nutrition has gone into our baby, when we can next anticipate the glorious freedom that their slumber allows us.

The autism mum faces years and years of this uncertainty, contrary to growing out of babyhood pickiness, her child becomes even more selective, even more adept at defying nature's incitement to surrender to the replenishing comfort of sleep.

We must keep reminding ourselves that autists are creatures of habit. When our children move on from the baby stage, where they are usually quite content to be spoon-fed nutrient packed slop, they tend to graduate to 'finger feeding'. Here our toddler discovers choice. They are in control of what goes into their mouths, how much, how long it takes to make their way through a meal. Conscious of the post meal mess that she will have to clean up, Mum tends to present bite sized dry offerings, and the resulting crumbs are efficiently sucked into the hoover, leaving no smears, spillages or stains.

And this is the stage at which many of our habitual little autists become stuck. When I talk to other autism mums about their children's selective eating habits, I hear over and over that the children are drawn to dry, brown foods, that they are disgusted by anything wet, or by different foods being mingled together. I hear that the youngster with autism tends to reject cutlery, even if he has the skill to use it; preferring to go 'au natural' and finger-feed. Coupled with the sensory differences that can manifest as an intense dislike of certain tastes and textures, I believe that this stagnation, this tendency to become trapped in a certain developmental stage is caused by the autist's lack of imagination.

It takes a leap of the imagination to try something new. Curiosity drives the typically developing child to take a look at what his parents or older siblings are eating, and to want to be part of the grown up world. A desire to please and to be admired can motivate a young child to act in ways that he believes will impress his parents. For the child with autism, loving the familiar, mistrustful of change, lacking typical curiosity or the desire to impress; the incentive to move on from his dry toast quarters, his chicken dippers and his tepid hash browns may just not be there.

When our children are young, and we are very conscious of all of the calories and nutrients necessary to build their growing bodies, these feeding problems weigh heavily on our minds. As the child grows, Mum gets used to his very particular eating habits. The years go by and the list of what her little one is prepared to accept as edible slowly becomes a little longer. If we're lucky, it becomes possible to assemble real, socially acceptable meals from the bank of permitted ingredients. Mum sees for herself as the weeks turn into months and the months turn into years that her child doesn't waste away, that he grows taller and stronger in just the same way as regular children do. Only with experience does she learn that despite his picky appetite, he manages quite well on this limited diet of his own design.

Of course, even the seasoned autism mum's pulse will start to quicken when one day, right out of the blue, her teenager decides to throw caution to the wind, to pull back his lips and tentatively test the texture of a green pepper against his teeth. We learn to never give up, because, just occasionally, miracles do happen!

Possibly, though, your friend has not reached this stage of resigned acceptance. The odds are that a battle of wills between mother and child is already well underway. This battle could rage on for many years, and her child's single minded determination to only allow certain textures, colours, brands, shapes or flavours past his lips is evenly matched by her purposeful resolve to get the nourishment that he needs to survive into his digestive system, by hook or by crook.

To crank up the urgency of the situation a notch or ten, she has the combined voices of social workers, health visitors, government ministers and dinner ladies ringing in her ears. Five-a-day becomes seven a day; gluten is suddenly a no-no, as is his all-time favourite, milk! Try cutting these two essentials, flour and dairy, from a picky eater's diet and despair at the lonely, unappetising produce that remains. Feeding advice galore comes from your friend's mother-in-law, sister-in-law, 'Supernanny' style gurus lecture in stern voices from the television set. She is assaulted with advice and instruction from anyone who cares to throw on their two-penneth. Sometimes I wonder, what is it about being a mum that invites people to lecture, advise and criticise? Each week as she empties the over-ripe contents of her fruit-bowl into the kitchen bin, her heart sinks. She becomes familiar with a growing sense of foreboding.

So, if your friend's child has firmly taken up camp in the culinary wilderness of turkey dinosaurs and Thomas the Tank yogurts, and if he seems unwilling or unable to summon up interest in any other foodstuffs, then feel free to share with her the story of my family and their various dietry fads, from the point of view of the chief cook and bottle washer (me!).

Our story is sure to make her feel a bit better. It may make her laugh, but mostly, I hope that it will give her some hope for the future.

***

As babies, my children were all champion eaters. I prided myself on my home-made mush, which I would shovel contentedly into the eager, wide-open mouths of my hungry little chicks. I was happy in the knowledge that this smooth, bland slop contained elements of every mineral, vitamin, every trace of protein and carbohydrate necessary for my babies' optimum development. Back then, I would even pass on my baby food recipes to dubious looking friends. In fact, I seriously considered writing a weaning recipe book as I was convinced that there was a gap in the market. Now, of course, I realise that that gap can be filled with a single sentence – 'boil, blend and spoon in,' but you know how irritatingly enthusiastic new mothers can be.

'The family that eats together, stays together' the old adage advises, and I enthusiastically adopted this advice as my mantra.

In my early twenties, eagerly anticipating family life, it was always the idea of mealtimes that captured my imagination. In my mind's eye I saw a brood of strapping boys (all wearing dungarees, for some reason). These varying sized, athletic looking specimens all reached to help themselves to the home-cooked bounty spread before them. Broths, stews and steaming pies, home baked bread with creamy yellow butter. To satisfy the healthy appetites, there would be cakes and fruit for afters. The youngest of this denim clad crew would fall to sleep on my lap as the cheese board was brought out. Endless courses, bountiful abundance. My idea of a vital, thriving family centred firmly on the food that would sustain it.

Despite the odds stacked against us, I still enforce the rule that my family eat together whenever possible. I love the feeling of being surrounded by my nearest and dearest, providing good, wholesome food to delight them and keep them healthy. The stuff that my family is eating, however, and the enthusiasm with which it goes down the hatch, is a far cry from those early rose-tinted vision of domestic bliss.

My husband is a type 1 diabetic (not his fault, I know, but I'm just saying). Rosie straddles the boundary lines between strict veganism and vegetarianism, occasionally leaping into the domain of desperate blood-thirsty carnivore, depending on her mood and level of hunger at any given mealtime.

Daisy, at fifteen, is still a fan of the mushed together slop that she ate in infancy, though its consistency is more chewable, and the ingredients a little saltier, spicier or cheesier.

Lenny is a super-wary finger-feeder, carefully selecting only the driest, beigest and blandest of foods. These all but tasteless provisions must be appropriately spaced on his dinner plate, untouched by any fellow foodstuffs. Any new introductions of the culinary variety are given the silent treatment, conscientiously objected to; viewed only fleeting out of the side of his eye. Expertly, he feels his way around them, dropping any unfamiliar items to the floor to be gobbled up instantly by our black and white greyhound, Delilah.

Oh, and then there is me, the greedy, food-obsessed architect of these daily rendezvous.

Not that I am complaining. It took many years of (sometimes gentle, sometimes dictatorial) encouragement before Lenny would even join us for a meal. In the early days he would roost beneath the table, nibbling at a Yorkshire pudding or a piece of breaded chicken. Way back, before this stage, I recall that he would spend mealtimes running naked up and down the dining room as I followed, sneaking morsels into his mouth like a determined mother hen. Nowadays, to see Lenny loitering with the family (always standing; to go so far as to place a single cheek of his bottom on his allotted seat would perhaps be a step too near commitment), sneaking suspicious glances at his dry, brown offerings and taking the occasional begrudging bite, well, this fills me with a glow of maternal satisfaction.

Daisy is a grabber. Like her mum, she loves to eat. Unfortunately, she makes no distinction between her own plate of food and the next person's. At mealtimes, her wheelchair is brought to the table and her lap-belt securely fastened. This is not entirely legal, I am told. Being restrained in any way, even for the duration of a Sunday roast, and even if the restrainee is deliriously happy, is a compromise of human rights. If anyone is able to offer a workable alternative, then, genuinely, I am all ears. Until that time, I am happy to continue to compromise Daisy's right to wander off mid-meal, or to plunge her hand into an oven-hot shepherd's pie.

Her mushed up version of the family meal is spoon or fork-fed to her, allowing lots of time for chewing and swallowing. Daisy has to be seated just over arms-length away from the table, to avoid the lighting fast thievery that could cause a dinnertime revolution. Even with this extra time for chewing and swallowing, she tends to store food, hamster-style, releasing a masticated glob the moment she is offered a drink. This offensive by-product must then be swiftly spirited away to avoid offence to other diners.

Of course, it is not only nutritional diligence that drives me to encourage the ritual of our family get-together at the

141

end of each day. I hate the thought of TV dinners, of each family member's daily experiences remaining unshared, while instead the focal point of the meal becomes the fictional goings on of unconvincing soap characters.

Because Daisy is non-verbal, I often volunteer snippets from her home-school diary to provide a glimpse into her 'world away from the family.' For instance; 'Daisy's enjoyed horse-riding today, everyone. She went four times around the paddock and then helped to groom Cinders!' This clumsy rounding up of her daily news is my way of keeping her involved in the family chatter. In all probability, she doesn't understand our words, but I am sure that, by the tone of our voices and the fact that we're looking directly at her when we speak about her school-time antics, she knows that she is very much a valued part of the family.

Lenny answers direct questions randomly, choosing his response from his repertoire of learned phrases. The answer that he gives often bears no relevance to the question.

'What did you do at school today, Lenny?'

'Tiger!'

'Have you been learning about tigers at school?'

'Bob the Builder!'

'Oh, did you sing 'Bob the Builder' at school?'

'Yogurt!'

'Do you want a yogurt?'

'Ice-cream!'

We get to the point eventually, even if the point for Lenny is far adrift from any original line of questioning. He loves to be involved though, and, for us, the pleasure of hearing his voice far outweighs the considerable effort that it takes to rope him in.

Rose is a teenager with Asperger's, so unless she is on the mood to converse (a joyous turn of events, bringing a carnival atmosphere in its wake) her input can be limited. And Richard is a man, so...

But valiantly, I continue! Each day a variety of dishes are rustled up, mushed up, spaced neatly apart on plates next to a ramekin of ketchup, and the painstaking game of conversational show and tell is played out over and over again.

I must say, though, my efforts are paying off. Who would imagine that an off-the-wall family like mine could regularly, and without too many alarming incidents, eat out in restaurants, or join in group picnics in the summertime? The key is nothing more than my acquiescence, my willingness to accept, to smile, to let go of that unrealistic, rose-tinted image of family life, and to enjoy what we have.

***

Among the wonderfully unique autists I have met along the way on my journey as an autism mum and advocate is a young man of twenty-one who adheres strictly to a diet of Shreddies, marmite on toast and dairy milk chocolate. His skin and eyes are beautifully clear, he is largely healthy, is always alert and interested in his environment. His mum (a close friend of mine) gave up trying to introduce new foods many years ago and has avoided much unhappiness because of her easy-going attitude. I've learned a lot from her. I know a four-year-old who survives on nothing but Yorkshire puddings and vitamin enriched drinks. I know many children who stick faithfully to trusted brands, completely unconvinced by underhand trickery such as slipping supermarket brand foods into the acceptable packaging of their favourites.

Through the special education schools that Daisy and Lenny have attended over the years, I also know many children who never eat at all, who are tube fed through their noses, or directly into their tummies. This doesn't seem to affect their lives negatively. In fact, many parents report that after the switch to a direct feeding method, then their child's overall health quickly improves. Choking hazards are reduced to a minimum and the surety that the child is getting everything he needs via the formula enables everyone to relax.

The story of our family mealtimes may seem bizarre, or may be too near the knuckle to share with your friend at the moment. My point, though, is that a relaxed attitude towards mealtimes is at least as important as the type of food being ingested. A happy family atmosphere is more valuable than any outsider's opinion of whether things are being done correctly.

I hope that after experiencing our mealtime vicariously, you will be able to shrug off your friend's concern about her little one's pickiness. Very selective eating can be a phase, or it can herald the beginning of a ritual that is played out through the autist's life. Either way, stress or bloody minded determination will only exacerbate the situation.

A speech-therapist once told me that taste-buds die off as we get older, and that most very young children are sensitive to strong flavours. We must also constantly remind ourselves that because of the differences in processing sensory information, people with autism are often experiencing something very differently than the neurotypical person does.

Some years ago, while watching me determinedly trying to coax Lenny to try a slice of banana, Rosie pointedly asked me, 'How would you feel if someone tried to make you to eat a slug?' This stopped me in my tracks, and I have never forgotten her analogy.

As your friend begins to realise that her child is quite able to survive on his chosen diet, I am sure that she, too, will begin to relax. There is no need for her validity as a parent to be judged by the structure of her family mealtimes, or even by the contents of her son's lunchbox. We can only do our best with whatever situation that we have, and sometimes doing our best means choosing to accept that things are what they are.

With your help, your friend will come to this realisation at an earlier junction than I did, and she will be able to sit, guilt and stress free, providing the vital example of enjoying her own meals while her family tuck into theirs.

Feats of Escapology, and the Associated Stress

Lenny, at fourteen, is an accomplished escapologist. Our wizard boy has an unnerving tendency to vanish. Not that Lenny in anyway dislikes his home or family; I believe that he loves us completely; his crushing hugs and gentle caresses express his feelings more eloquently than words could ever hope to.

Our boy longs for the big wide world. He is far less content than typical boys of his age to remain indoors (most of my friends complain about the difficulty they have detaching their teenage sons from the lifeline of their gaming consoles) but ironically, he has much less opportunity for the freedom he desires. Once free from the oppressive stuffiness of indoor life, he is blind to the dangers that his parents see on every stretch of road, in every lake and river, and in the motives of every friendly stranger.

Lenny is constantly beckoned to the outdoor world, by his mistress, the great love of his life, Mother Nature.

He was only two years old when we he first gave us the fright of our lives by wandering off. On a holiday in

Minorca, with a cluster of three villas taken over by our extended family, we spent the first few days of a two-week holiday relaxing in a state of bliss, as our children were more than content to play with their cousins in the sundrenched garden and private pool, which was securely surrounded by a high privet hedge.

Such tranquillity can only be enjoyed for so long, and by the fourth day the children were starting to become a little restless. We took a bus ride to a local beach, which we were alarmed to discover was absolutely choc-a-block with tourists. We staked our claim to an eight-foot square patch of sand, laid out our towels, sun screen and other holiday paraphernalia, and worked out a system by which we could both enjoy a little relaxation. We took it in turns to keep a close eye on the children, while one of us read a book or had a little nap in the sun.

After the event, neither Richard nor I could put our finger on exactly what went wrong with this fool-proof system, but some point mid-afternoon we noticed that Lenny was missing. Calmly at first, we agreed that I would stay with the girls while Richard jogged around the beach, in every increasing circles, asking people along the way to look out for a two-year-old in red trunks and a green, tied on sun hat.

The panic quickly escalated. With every minute that Lenny was gone the situation became more alarming. Soon the whole beach was looking for him. A German with a loudspeaker was issuing a description of him, and a plea for anyone who spotted our toddler to keep him safe until he could be reunited with us. How incredibly long a period of twenty-five minutes can seem, when your non-verbal toddler has gone AWOL.

He was eventually found in the doorway of a restaurant, where a decorative gushing fountain held him in awe-struck captivity. Rich had walked past the fountain several times in his desperate searching spiral. He had been continually shouting his name, but, worryingly, Lenny had failed to respond. He either did not recognise his own name, or was so distracted by the beauty of the spurting fountain that he was deaf to his father's calls. I lost the strength in my legs when he was eventually handed over to me in one piece. I sat on the beach holding him saying his name over and over, but Lenny was oblivious to my distress, or my relief, and simply reached for his beaker of juice.

Over the years there have been many such instances of escapology, and Lenny has only become more adept at breaking out or breaking way. He could scale the eight-foot fence surrounding our fully enclosed back garden at seven years old. Our little garden backs on to a series of neighbouring plots, all surrounded by similar fencing. Being alerted to the fact that he was missing, I once watched from my bedroom window as my seven-year-old son vaulted over this series of fences with the graceful ease of an Olympic athlete. Rich had gone to our neighbour's to retrieve him, but I hollered from the bedroom window that Lenny was now six gardens ahead of the game.

Then he needs constant supervision, do I hear you say? Of course, over time we began to realise that Lenny would take off at any given opportunity. We increased our security, upgrading every few years or so to the supposedly fool-proof system that we have in place today. Still, though, I see Lenny glance, quick and sly as a fox, at the door every time someone enters or exits. With this quick-as-a-flash appraisal he is on the look-out for that inevitable opportunity, the occasion when we are distracted by a ringing phone, a crying sister or some other commotion. He is cunning enough to sit on his knowledge of the unlocked door for a while, until any interfering adults are well out of sight and earshot, and then he will be off.

The risk-assessment that must be updated every six months at Lenny's respite placement recently described him as an 'Opportunist Bolter, which I thought made him sound like a shady criminal or a fox.

One of the most upsetting break-out incidents happened when Richard had just returned from work last summer, his mobile phone had momentarily distracted him from adequately applying the system of locks. This time, Lenny didn't go far, and as soon as I noticed that he was out, I sternly ordered that he come in from the small patch of front garden, where he was happily playing with some pebbles. Locks were re-applied and we all went about our business. Only ten minutes after that, when there was a frantic knocking at our front door, did we discover that when he had escaped, Lenny had also let Daisy out into the street. There she sat, also playing with pebbles, but in the middle of the road.

A few days later we received a call from social services. The incident had been reported by our neighbour, and my family worker wanted to visit immediately, in order to discuss security and the general supervision of our kids. I was gutted on both counts. The fact that Daisy had been in such danger, and the fact that one of our neighbours could have cruelly used this incident as a weapon against us. I felt peeved with our family worker when she arrived; up until that time I had considered her a family friend, there to advise me of services and to facilitate the children's review meetings. Yet here she was with a colleague that I had never met before, behaviour stiffly professional, insisting that I explain myself.

I felt doubly betrayed and victimised.

After the shock of these sequence of events had worn off, though, I was forced to re-evaluate the scenario. What would I have done if I had found an unsupervised, pyjama-clad toddler in the middle of a busy road? (Daisy has a learning age of approximately eighteen months, so, when it comes to her personal safety and her awareness of dangers, this comparison is a fair one).

Without the skills or the authority to challenge the situation myself, I would certainly have had to alert someone with the power to investigate, and to act if necessary. And my family worker had only been doing the job for which she is paid; in fact, the final result of the referral was that services were able to provide an even more effective security system, and even offered to supply an extra pair of hands, to entertain the children for an hour as I prepared tea. I peevishly declined this extra help, feeling paranoid about being spied on, but in the end decided to accept that nobody was working against me, or to punish me. There is a system in place to offer protection and assistance for families like ours, and Lenny's escape had merely triggered this system into action.

Regardless of any security system, the constant threat of Lenny's desire to escape is a pressure that adds an extra layer of stress to our already full-on lives. I often awake from disturbing dreams, heart thumping, shouting my son's name. I compulsively check that he is safely in his room. Lenny's constant contented humming acts as a type of radar, and if he is out of the range of my vision, I can usually determine exactly where he is within the house. I have learned to correlate his distinctive sounds to certain activities, and can easily recognise the delighted humming sound that he makes when he is doing something disruptive.

This constant, almost unconscious assessment of his noises in order to locate and ascertain what he is up to seems to take no effort on my part; it has become second nature. Or at least I assume it has, until the time when he is in respite and then the quietness of the house, the way that I am able to relax to a deeper level without having to continuously be aware of the threat of escape or destruction; this highlights the raised state of alertness that it is necessary for us all to be in whenever Lenny is home.

Only last week, Lenny and I were up early so I decided that it would be nice to make a flask of coffee, take our dog for an early morning walk and treat ourselves to the spectacle of the spring sunrise. Richard had already left for work, and Daisy was sound asleep. I had heard Rosie stirring in her attic room, so I shouted up to her, letting her know that I was taking the dog out for a walk, and asked her to keep an ear out for Daisy waking up.

Still half asleep, Rosie had misunderstood, assuming that both her brother and sister were still asleep in their beds. She got up soon after we left, and checked both of their rooms. Daisy still slept soundly, but she found Lenny's room completely empty. Still in her pyjamas, wearing her Dad's trainers (the first footwear that she could lay her hands on) she ran out of the house, calling Lenny's name. Fortunately, one of the neighbours had already seen me with Lenny walking our dog so Rosie's fears were allayed pretty swiftly. This was her start to the day, though.

Sometimes I reflect on how unfair the situation is; Richard and I are adults, and even for us the pressure is sometimes unbearable. For a sensitive, thoughtful young person like Rosie, I can only guess at the effects of living with such responsibility. Even in our sleep, we are constantly aware of the possibility that our boy can, and will, break out whenever he finds and opportunity to do so.

There have also been a few false alarms; one time Lenny hid out in the airing cupboard, standing silently, a sentinel guarding the emptiness of his hidey-hole for the best part of an hour. We searched every room, shouting his name all the while, reasoning that he could not have got out of the house, all doors being bolted and all windows safely screwed down. I'm not sure what prompted me to open the airing cupboard door in my search for him; desperation I guess, or maybe some maternal sixth sense, but I still remember the look of absolute surprise on his face when I eventually found him.

Lenny used to enjoy sitting in our car, which is parked on the road, directly in front of the living room window. He would happily listen to music, playing the same track over and over again. This suited us all, as we weren't subjected to the wearing loop of repeated music that he loves so much. We were able to keep an eye on him, happily rocking back and forth to his fractured music in the cosy confines of the parked car. This practice had to abruptly stop, though, when one day an inevitable diversion (I can't quite remember what) caused me to take my eye off my son's head-banging silhouetted profile for a moment, and the next time I looked, he had gone. Another emergency search, with his most likely destination (the biscuit aisle of the Co-op) being ruled out first.

Richard grabbed the car keys and took off, driving round and around our village while I stayed at home to look after my girls. On this occasion, Lenny had hopped from the front seat of our boringly average Zafira, into a smart white soft-top convertible that was parked in our neighbour's yard. He was very happily trying out these new, much classier wheels, but, as the neighbour who brought him home reported, seemed a little disappointed by the fact that her classic car had no CD player.

Another time he had holed up in the guinea-pigs' stone-built miniature house which is in our back garden. I could hear Lenny's constant contented hum, but, frustratingly, could not find him. A quick search of our neighbour's garden didn't bring the expected results. Where was he? Another flash of inspiration and I swung open the removable rooftop panel, to find Lenny, squatting amid the sawdust, three brown guinea-pigs cowering in the corners, surprised by the arrival of their gigantic roomy.

I am not alone in having to constantly supervise a runaway child, I know. My friend's teenage boy once went missing overnight. He is a very capable communicator and traveller. At a fleeting glance, nothing about him would alert a stranger to the fact that he is autistic and that he should not be out alone. Like many autists, he has a love of trains, and a fascination with schedules and journey planning. Without so much as a penny in cash about his person, he had hopped on a train to London to take in the bright city lights. It was a terrible night, my friend was distraught, and I still feel sick when I hear the whirr of the police helicopter. The sound takes me straight back to that long, long night, when I lay in bed waiting for news and listening to the helicopter hovering around and around the village in an all-night search for our missing friend.

If I could change one thing about the everyday workings of our family life, I would remove this constant threat of escape and disaster. It means that Richard, Rosie and I are in constant flight or fight mode, always ready to respond to an emergency situation. This, I believe, is extremely detrimental to emotional health. It is one of the hardest things that we have to live with, and directly or indirectly, is the cause of much of the tension within my marriage.

Relationship Pressures

At various support groups, at my children's schools, and as I strike up conversations with people generally, I come into contact with more and more mothers who are going it alone, either by choice or because circumstance dictates that they have no other option. This troubles me greatly. I know how ridiculously difficult life can be for me, and I have a partner who can support me emotionally, financially, and who gives a whole lot of help with the practical side of parenting. I cannot imagine how these single mums are managing to juggle everything that life throws at them, while also parenting a child with autism.

I believe that any resources poured into supporting the marriages of those of us with autistic children represents money well spent. Parenting courses, marital guidance, respite resources and grants for specialist holidays or extra services – the amount of government money dedicated to this support will easily be offset if marriages are supported to stay strong, and if mum and dad are able to stay together. If the human cost of a marital break-up is not enough to persuade those in power to invest in our marriages, then the financial implications of a split should add reasonable weight to the argument.

Having a child with any form of special need can put a couple's relationship under incredible pressure, and if there are already cracks in that relationship, then this pressure can very quickly dissolve the unstable marriage or partnership. Forgive me if this seems to be a gloomy outlook, but unfortunately it is nothing but the truth. The statistics speak for themselves.

Even the strongest of unions will be tested.

I am very lucky to have a wonderful husband. Actually, it is much more good management than luck. Richard is an amazing father, always willing to take the children out on adventures, braving activities that I would cowardly shrink back from. I have learned so much from him over the years. In many ways he is braver than me, willing to take small risks with the children. These are never risks that could result in any serious consequence, but he will happily try something new, whereas I usually opt to go back to tried and tested activities and places, where I know from past experience that I am able to cope.

His optimistic outlook means that he constantly expects more of the children, he gives them a little responsibility and is prepared to put effort into pushing the boundaries of their autonomy. I try to plan for every eventuality, my rampant imagination taunting me with detailed images of everything that could possibly go wrong throughout the course of an outing. I often talk myself out of something before we have even got going, choosing instead to drive the children to a familiar restaurant, and to spin the meal out for a couple of hours or so.

Richard and I have very different methods, and I frequently hold my hands in the air and admit that his are not only braver but often far more effective than mine.

Over the years though, our different approaches towards parenting have been the root of some very distressing fall-outs. We are both fairly reasonable people, both happy to step back from an argument that might prove destructive. Together, we have learned to put our marriage and the happy atmosphere within our family home ahead of any small personal victory. When it comes to important decisions regarding the children's well-being and education though, it is much more difficult to 'throw' the battle.

Despite the fact that nine-year-old Rosie had clearly recognised her own autistic traits, was unfazed by the fact that she was on the spectrum, and had gone out of her way to ask us to put her forward for diagnosis, Richard was unsure that this was the way to go.

In his eyes, Rosie was perfect. He was less familiar with the subtler presentations of autism than I was, and found it difficult to believe that this intelligent, funny, communicative child could really be disabled. He sat on his misgivings throughout the long assessment process, but I sensed a reluctance to attend the various meetings that we had with educational psychologists, speech therapists and paediatricians. He didn't even seem to be willing to discuss what went on in the meetings. On the evening before we were due to hear the experts' final decision, I noticed that he was unusually tense.

'Do you need to get something off your chest?' I asked, tentatively.

With a little coaxing and persuasion, he told me what had been running through his mind. He thought that if the conclusion was positive, if the multidisciplinary panel considered that Rosie did have autism, then we should tell her that they had come to the opposite conclusion. Whatever the outcome, we should lead her to believe that she wasn't autistic.

I was horrified. Lie to my daughter about something that affected her so fundamentally? How could we even consider it? Not wanting to react straight away, I stalled for time, taking Daisy on a supermarket shopping trip, in order to get my thoughts and responses in order. I arrived back later that night, armed with bread, fruit and veg, and my carefully thought out opposition.

I urged him to have a bit of foresight, to look ahead to the future when Rosie would reach the age of eighteen and have access to her own medical records. How would she feel once she realised that her whole childhood had been built on a lie?

The argument quickly became heated. Richard struggled to remain patient and in control, as he explained his theory that what children believe about themselves solidifies, becomes their own personal truth. Tell someone that they are well, they are normal, that they don't particularly need special treatment or to be afforded special privileges, and they will happily adopt this version of reality. Tell that same person that they are weak, vulnerable, that they are in some way less than their peers, and this is incorporated into their belief system.

My counter-argument was again that one day she would find out that she had been autistic all along. She was (and is) an incredibly bright young lady. For God's sake, she had already worked it out! Even if we were able to convince her that her incredibly perceptive self-diagnosis wasn't a hit, and even if we were able to keep up this lie for the next nine years, then her eventual discovery of the truth would be inevitable. What would that tell her about our attitude to autism, to disability? That her condition was so unacceptable to us, so repugnant, that we thought it better to re-write history and make long-term professional liars of ourselves rather than embrace her difference?

The disagreement raged on, our points of view being expressed through vehement whispers, in an effort not to distress the children.

Most differences of opinion can be resolved somewhere on the neutral ground of compromise, but in this situation there only seemed to be two options, to tell her the truth or to lie.

Sick with worry I stayed awake for most of the night, progressing and re-living the horrible argument through occasional fractured dreams. The next day, with Richard at work and the children at school, I attended the appointment and was quickly told that the professionals all agreed that Rosie did, in fact, have Asperger's Syndrome. Their decision was unanimous, cut and dried. Mostly because it would lead to the only possible amicable solution to our disagreement, I had been praying that the clinical experts would come back with a 'no.' Bleary eyed from lack of sleep, I felt too emotionally drained to face another conflict, so I texted Richard to pass on their conclusion.

That night at dinner, with all of us present, I brought up the dreaded subject.

'Hey, Rosie, I went to the meeting today, you know about your autism diagnosis?'

'And what do they think? Do I have it?' she asked casually, between forkfuls.

I glanced at Richard and he gave an almost imperceptible nod of the head.

'They said that, yes, you have Asperger's Syndrome.'

'Wooo!' Rosie punched the air in celebration of the news. When I asked her why she was so happy she said that now she wasn't the only child in the family without a disability. Despite Richard's misgivings, this brought a small smile to his face.

The reason for highlighting this brief time of conflict in our marriage is not to portray either parent as the baddy, nor is it to create a public opportunity for me to bask in the glory of my right decision. I do believe that I was right to be frank and open with Rosie, but there are always many different ways to look at any situation. Richard did have a point, and that point was made because of his overpowering love for his daughter, and his desire for her to have a stable and trouble-free future.

In this instance, we did things my way. That is not to say that I completely disregarded my husband's misgivings. I agreed that it would not be wise to tell Rosie that she was disabled, that we should never suggest there was any goal or achievement that was beyond her capabilities. We made a decision then that we would only ever talk about the children in a positive light, and that would be the case whether they were present or not. We would focus on their talents, and abilities. In this stance, we would not deny the conditions that were part and parcel of who they were, but we would become mindful optimists, choosing to manifest potential instead of incapacity.

To be completely fair to him, there have been times in the past nine years when Rosie has used her diagnosis to get out of doing certain things or as an excuse to act in a particular (immature) way. However gifted and sharp, however much of a brilliant, out-of-the-box thinker she is, children are children, and from time to time are wont to use everything and anything at their disposal as a tool to manipulate a situation to their own advantage.

An earlier disagreement that we were able to work through with a much more amicable solution concerned Daisy and our choice of educational setting for her. At nearly three years old it was time for Daisy to enter the world of formal education. Because she couldn't walk, and because I saw her as being so very vulnerable, she had, until that time, spent almost every waking moment attached to my hip. Daisy was still very much my baby.

The thought of my sticky, sickly baby spending her days in the care of someone else, somebody who was unfamiliar with her quirks, and might not necessarily be completely attentive or completely attuned to her unspoken needs, was alarming. Richard took a more practical stance, and his casual research told him that children with special needs ultimately achieved better outcomes if they were placed in a 'normal' setting. In this case, he was pushing for mainstream school.

In the meantime, my elder sister and I took a trip to the nearest special school, which was located only six miles from our village. My sister had been a special needs nurse working with disabled adults for many years, and I was very keen for her to accompany me to give her view on the quality of the provision. We were shown around the facilities, and I made an instant connection with Chris, a very experienced special needs teacher, who at that time, was in charge of the 'early years' school nursery.

Used to seeing Daisy as being very dependent in comparison with my two other children, my nieces and nephews and my children's friends, I was laid bare by my first encounter with children who were attached to complex feeding, breathing and mobility equipment. Here for the first time I met children who were not necessarily expected to make it to adulthood. It was a surreal experience. A whole new world had suddenly opened up before my very eyes. I had gently, tentatively pushed a door which had swung open to allow access to a touching, disturbing dimension. It was a world full of vibrant, dynamic characters who required the most thorough, tender care imaginable. I felt sure that my sweet, golden haired Daisy, my baby, would very soon become part of this world. Here, Daisy would receive specialised nursing, have access to physiotherapy, hydrotherapy, occupational therapy and the most up-to-date specialised teaching expertise.

Overcome with emotion, I didn't need very much persuasion. This was the place where Daisy belonged, this was a place where she could remain protected, be gently nurtured, and enjoy the benefits of a peaceful, unchallenged infancy.

My mood when I came home was reflective, distant, but resigned.

My husband had other ideas.

He was sure that Daisy shouldn't remain unchallenged. She need not exist in an 'outside society' otherworld where comfort and tranquillity were priorities. She was going to grow up, and she would become an adult with as much independence as could be afforded to her. There was every chance that she would learn to walk, to speak, to make decisions for herself. Why was I adopting this negative stance, giving up on her so early in the game?

Our different perspectives equated to a deadlock. Richard saw a wonderful, independent future for Daisy where I saw only vulnerability, danger, and death. It may have been my inherent pessimism, or it may have been the result of emotional damage incurred through the insensitive care I received after Daisy's birth, but I simply did not dare entrust my precious, defenceless angel to the coarse, cut-throat world of mainstream education.

It was Alison, one of the school nurses at the special school I had visited, and a friend from our village, who suggested a dual placement for Daisy. I had never imagined this as an achievable outcome – it just hadn't occurred to me. Using our best cooperation skills, Rich and I sat down and listed the benefits of each school setting. To set it out on paper and review the options in this way was far more productive than to argue the point. When the problem was set out in black and white, we could both see that there were clear advantages to each setting. If she were to attend the local primary school alongside her older sister, Daisy would have a place in our community. School really is the centre of the community – I have met all of my closest friends through the schools that my children attended. Despite my reservations about the danger that mainstream school might present, I very much wanted Daisy to stake her place in our friendly little village.

Our plan for a dual placement met with some resistance. Both schools were on board straight away, and seemed to agree that, for Daisy, there could be no better option. The deputy head of the local primary school, who was also Rosie's class teacher at the time, was a keen supporter of inclusion, 'Bring it on!' she told me, enthusiastically, when news that we had made the application reached her. She felt that not only would the inclusive placement be good for Daisy, but the other children would gain value from getting to know, respect and befriending a pupil with a severe learning disability.

It was an exciting prospect. With the dual placement, Daisy would have access to all of the facilities in special school and enjoy the benefit of truly belonging to our village.

The resistance to our plan came from the local education authority. I had a few heated exchanges on the telephone with an LEA professional who assured me that she had no superior with whom I could negotiate. I knew from my repeated attempts to get hold of this woman that she only worked two days out of the week, and I expressed my surprise at the possibility that someone who worked on such a part-time basis could really be the top dog. My sarcasm was not received gracefully. She dug her heels in and said that there was no way that a dual placement would be granted for my daughter. The reason for her knock-back was vague, 'Our system isn't set up for something like that. You choose one school, or you choose another. That's the way it works.'

I had met with my first example of bloody minded obstinacy. On my journey as a special needs mum I would meet with many, many more examples of this kind of lack of flexibility, so, looking back I see now that this challenge was good training for me. I was furious! My fury was mostly as a result of the fact that I had felt so relieved, so joyous, so proud when Richard and I were able quickly arrive at an amicable compromise. We were grown-ups!

We could do this parenting thing! The fact that this faceless individual on the other end of the telephone could simply say 'no way' without giving the matter due consideration made me feel deeply angry.

My weapon of choice was the pen (or, more accurately, the laptop) and I wrote a detailed, concise account of all of the reasons that we felt Daisy would benefit from a dual placement. If the system wasn't set up for such a compromise, then we would force the powers that be to challenge the system. The list read quite dryly. I felt I needed to inject a bit of emotion to get people on our side. I began with a paragraph about Daisy, about how much she meant to us, about how sickly she had been in her early life. Then I added a paragraph about our hopes for her future, about our wider hopes for complete integration, a knitting together of society that would benefit all concerned. I issued a plea to the reader of this letter to get behind me, to make that leap of faith, to get behind positive change-making and to show the rest of the world by example how things should be done.

After these emotive paragraphs, I slotted in the much more practical reasons why it would be good for Daisy to spend two days in mainstream school, and the remainder of the week in a special educational setting.

My letter was good! I could tell, because when I gave it to my friends for an experimental read through, they either started to cry or wanted to start a revolution. It was rousing, emotive, and, above all, it was convincing, reasonable and balanced. I started to feel that, despite the LEA's confident dismissal of our proposal, perhaps we had some power after all.

I copied the letter a dozen times and sent it to Daisy's paediatrician and to the heads and governors of both schools. I sent it to our local MP, Daisy's physiotherapist, a copy each for Joyce and Barbara, my portage workers. I sent copies to anyone I felt could add weight to my argument. Lo and behold within a few days of posting I received a call from the head of our local Primary School. He told me that he would make sure that the dual placement went ahead. He had liaised with the head of the special school, and they would push the LEA to agree our case. Fully-inclusive education, dual placements, and all forms of inclusion were the way to go, he was convinced.

We felt empowered and supported – we had worked together as a team, not only to find an agreeable solution to our dilemma but also to forge a little change. Together, we were mighty, and that felt so good.

Daisy's dual placement did go ahead, and remained in place throughout the course of her primary school education. She thoroughly enjoyed her time at both settings. In mainstream school she was supported by Miss Parker, a teaching assistant with whom she developed a wonderful bond. Miss Parker remains a close family friend to this day. We often chat about those days that Daisy spent in Primary School. To the wonderful class that she grew up amongst, she was a princess. They had a club, 'The Daisy Club,' each member of the club would wear a paper Daisy in their cardigan buttonhole. The club would meet at playtime, and they would take turns to 'look after' Daisy, to pamper and entertain her. Sometimes I wondered if this was quite right, if Daisy should really grow up being pampered and adored by her peers in this way, but their hearts were in the right place and my little girl loved the attention.

On a memorable sports day in her mainstream setting, Daisy 'ran' the 100 metre race. She had just learned to walk at this time, her steps were slow and methodical, and she was supported by Miss Parker, who, with one arm around Daisy's waist, 'ran' the race alongside her. Of course, the other runners finished the race within moments, but the whole school cheered for Daisy as, laboriously, ecstatic smile on her face, she completed her run. I was not the only one overcome with emotion that day as chants of 'Dai-SY, Dai-SY rang in my ears. It was like the ending of a very cheesey movie. It is also one of the happiest memories that I treasure.

Daisy's time at special school was also going very well. Chris, the early years teacher, was as excellent as my first impressions of her had told me she would be, and she also became a family friend. She had an old fashioned 'no nonsense' approach, and valued practical things like ensuring that the kids in her class had healthy snacks, spent time outdoors, and were sent home in a clean and tidy condition. Chris was uber-practical; an engineer's daughter, she hated the over-priced merchandise sold by special needs companies, and would invent her own sensory toys to delight the children in her care. She would play music all the time in the classroom, anything from opera to S Club 7. The music changed constantly. She once told me that she felt that it was so important for these kids to be stimulated, to enjoy their school days, to be given a chance for a little bit of life outside the home or hospital, because, really, who knew how long they would be here for? Clearly, to Chris, her position as teacher and protector of her little class was so much more than just a job. Bringing these children on, and providing them with an oasis of normalcy was her calling.

***

I have offered two examples of marital clashes that we worked hard to overcome, one more satisfactorily than the other. They were by far the biggest disruptions in our marriage and really shook the status quo of our relationship. Because of stress, bone-deep tiredness, financial pressures and the constant necessity to clean up the messes made by my very sensory children, there have been times when we have fallen into the trap of bickering, taking our frustrations out on one another. Even though this bickering is unpleasant, I see its value within a marriage. When we are tired, frustrated or angry, we use one another as a buffer to absorb the frustration. This way, the children are spared the visitation of our wrath. After the spat, with a little space to reflect and recover, we both recognise the fact that we are under enormous pressure, we choose to be forgiving and reasonable. We know that the nature of our family life allows very little time for the rest and recuperation that is essential for a consistent, laid-back temperament.

Over time, though, this 'living on the edge' with very little sleep and very many challenges, takes its toll. Over the past five years, Richard and I have both required extra medical support for our mental health. Throughout the same period, we have both noticed a steep physical decline; I suffered two slipped discs in my back, regular digestive problems and headaches. He a short-term memory problem that leaves him frustrated and constantly searching for words that are on the 'tip of his tongue.' Without exception, the parents of disabled children that I know suffer greatly, physically, emotionally, and with their mental health. This is no coincidence; it's a tough road to travel.

As the years have gone by, we have both become very supportive of one another's 'extra-familiar activities.' We actively encourage one another to go away with friends for a few days at a time and to enjoy regular evenings out. We have reached the point where we recognise that this is absolutely essential. When either of us has been away or had a chance to experience something new, we come back refreshed, with extra energy, with a new take on things, and something to talk about. The only problem with this 'tag team parenting' is that we rarely get a chance to do things together. We are constantly evaluating, trying to get the balance right, and this is something that we've decided we need to work on now, as the children are getting older. Nowadays, Richard takes a day off work each month, and we go for a long walk together, followed by a nice lunch. It's not much in the grand scheme of things, but it does give us a chance to enjoy one another's company without the constant stress of having to keep an eye on the children.

If my message is clear and doing the job that I intended it to, these examples will leave you wondering if there is anything that you can do to support the marriage/relationship of your friend and her partner. The truth is this simple, in the long run it will be far better for her and her child if she is supported. When there are two parents to share the fun times and the challenges, life is better all round. Even when those two parents disagree on a key point, input from two different perspectives can be very valuable.

Now is the best time to start building that bond with your friend's child. You could start with an hour long outing, taking the youngster for a walk to the park. If you are the competent, caring person that I am sure you must be to have invested your time and energy reading my words, you will slowly be able to build this up, over the weeks and months. There is no reason why you would not be able to provide informal respite for your friend's child. One night a month will provide a wonderful opportunity for her to spend some quality time with her husband or partner. In a healthy family, the couple will spend time together. Each family member should also spend time away from the home, engaging in enriching activities. This applies to the children, as well as to Mum and Dad.

Make sure that you continue to arrange nights out with your friend. She may not be her pre-children, fun-loving self at the moment, but afford her a little forgiveness. She may resist your invitations, and if she does, please persist. Don't take 'no' for an answer. She may feel too tired to embark on a wild night of drinking and dancing, but any time away from the home, even just for a walk and a quiet drink in a country pub, will refresh her, and allow her to return to the bosom of her family with a new dynamism. If she has hidden her former, fun-loving self behind layers of sadness, then you can help her to let that old self out, even if it is just for an hour or so.

We mustn't forget Dad in all of this! His social life should be supported as well. Knowing that his wife is getting out regularly and enjoying the company of her friends will leave him free to enjoy the occasional guilt-free night out too. It's all about balance. The extra care that children with autism require can easily offset the natural balance of the family rhythm. Before we know it, we can begin to resent any time that our partner spends away from the pressures of family life, even though our common sense tells us that relief from that pressure is absolutely necessary for each parent, if a complete mental breakdown is to be avoided.

In the event of an unsolvable disagreement, a third party opinion can be useful. Your opinion is all the more valuable if you are able to remain unbiased and fair. At other times, all that we want from our friend is someone to listen and to validate our feelings of sadness or frustration. Often, after a little moan about a disagreement that we have had with our partner, the negative energy is released, and a few hours down the line we find that we don't even feel that bitterness or anger any more. With you on hand, as the friend who offers neutral advice, a shoulder to cry on, the friend who insists on occasional night out, your autism mum will benefit in so many ways. You can help to support her marriage to stay strong. It's a worthwhile investment of your time and energy, firstly, because she is your friend, and, without doubt, you want her to continue to be a part of your life. Secondly, because in the event that her marriage breaks down, she is going to need you a whole lot more!

Staying Well

Let me tell you everything that I have learned about staying well, mentally, emotionally and physically. Forgive me if some of my advice seems obvious, but often the simplest, most obvious adjustments that we make in our life are the ones that bring speedy, effective change.

Conscious as I am of my vital role in my children's lives, and of how much more effective I am when I am well, alert and positive, I am now, at forty-six years old, the keenest I have ever been to eat, sleep, meditate and exercise my way into becoming the best version of myself. As part of the autism awareness work that Rosie and I are involved in, I am now called upon to do quite a lot of travelling, and on top of the ongoing pressures of supporting my family, I pack a heck of a lot of work into my daytimes, evenings and weekends. One of the things that I have to constantly keep an eye on is that I am not taking too much on board. I tend to get very giddy about things, a surge of excitement overtakes my rational mind, and in such phases I truly believe that I can do anything at all. Of course this manic side of my personality has it's inevitable opposite, and at times I simply flump, exhausted and deflated like a let-down balloon.

Emotionally I have been up and down over the years. The gloomy, drawn-to-darkness child grew into a gloomy, drawn-to-darkness teenager and young woman. Pregnancy and marriage (yes; in that order) gave me a boost, allowed me to visit a contented place that I could never have imagined existed. Shortly after my babies were born, though, the pain of their diagnoses sucked me back again, to that familiar, dark terrain. I had tasted real happiness, though, and was determined to have more of the same. My sparkling vision of happy family life remained, always, it seemed, just out of my grasp. I have spent the last fifteen years or so determinedly ploughing on, resolutely trekking through my naturally depressive state in a bid to set up camp in that joyful place. Whatever challenges fate puts in my way, onwards I plough!

Physically, I am lucky enough to enjoy good health. I am very much aware, though, that our mental, physical and emotional wellbeing are inseparably intertwined, a rope of three threads with each twine drawing strength from the union. When we are sick emotionally, we soon become sick physically. When we endure a period of mental illness, our body and our relationships suffer. Everything is connected, and an appraisal of our general health should include intense scrutiny of the three separate strands, each being equally important in the fine balance of our wellbeing.

Mental or emotional disease tend to creep up on a person. There is usually no single trigger, or a point where we feel something 'go,' nor is there one particular day when we awake and decide that the fun things in life just aren't worth the effort. For me, the anticipation of fun is my absolute litmus test for good mental health. When I am planning ahead, visualising in great detail what to cook for a particular occasion, who to invite, what to wear, etc., I know that I am enjoying a period of robust emotional and mental health. When I'm in it, I can't imagine being out, I feel sure that the force will stay with me.

When nothing seems to run away with me, when I just can't seem to drum up the energy required to organise things, or to plan the fun aspects of our life, then it is time to take stock, and put some emergency measures into immediate action.

Because things can quickly go from bad to worse, especially in the case of someone facing major and unexpected changes, it will benefit your friend greatly if she learns to become 'in tune' with her own emotional health. It's not a giant drop from being unable to muster up the enthusiasm required to plan events, to not participating in events altogether, to spending one's days drearily plodding through mundane tasks with no vision, no joyful end in sight. From this stage, we can easily slip further still into the slippery mire of depression, where we give up on even these mundane tasks. From this dark place, it is no easy task to claw our way out. Depression can be quite a comfortable ditch to lie in, it is our cosy little hole and we find that we are alone with our dark thoughts, with no immediate plans to heave ourselves out. With our head turned to the damp earth, we can't see the sunlight above, we are deaf to the singing of the birds and the sound of children playing only yards from where we lay. We are aware of little but the familiar blanket of discontent that covers us.

Sorry, getting a little carried away with the old symbolism there!

It will serve your friend well if she adopts the habit of regularly 'scanning' her life for those give-away signs that all is not well. We are all vulnerable to the tides of emotion; it is part of the human condition.

If our emotions are like the weather, with dark clouds passing, sometimes staying for a while, and then moving on, then I like to imagine that, behind the clouds the sun is always shining, providing clues to its constant presence in the form of the glimmering silver edges that sometimes outline those rainclouds. Here's where the metaphor comes unstuck. There is very little that we can do about the bad weather; we can only remain hopeful and wait it out. To lift our mood is a little easier. I find its best to take a many angled approach, to make several small changes at once, and to wait for the magic to happen.

Here is a reminder of a basic check list for low mood. Answer 'yes' to more than a couple of these questions, and it really is time to take action.

1/ Do I sometimes or often experience feelings of guilt?

Guilt is a weird one. Once we become parents, guilt tends to have us well and truly in its clutches. As mums, we feel guilty if we work, we're not spending enough time with the children. We feel guilty if we don't work; our partner is carrying the weight of financial responsibility, we're not setting enough of a positive example for our children. The feeling of guilt can be almost comforting. It can sometimes seem that punishing ourselves with the constant grinding of guilt, for any past mistakes or misdemeanors, means that deep down, we are good. We have been bad, and because we recognise this, we feel bad, and so these two different layers of 'badness' cancel one another out. That may be the subconscious theory, but, in truth, there is nothing constructive about feeling guilty. It can stop us in our tracks, prevent action or growth. It is a very destructive, very undermining emotion, and to be able to recognise compulsive guilty thought processes is the first step towards stopping this torturous form of self-flagellation.

2/ Have my sleep and eating patterns changed dramatically?

Our mood and thought processes often affect our appetite and ability to sleep, and it is sudden changes in either of these areas that we must scan for. When feeling emotionally drained, I tend to retire early, yearning for the comfort of oblivion, but always wake in the early hours, with my thoughts racing and the soothing balm of sleep eluding me. Depressed people can sleep more or less than they used to when they were well. Similarly, a sudden loss of weight, or a dramatic weight gain can be triggered by depression.

3/ Do I feel sad, empty, or often burst into tears?

Crying in itself is a valid form of self-expression, and if your friend has been upset by the recent developments in her family life, it may be that frequent bursts of emotional outpourings are a very natural, very healthy coping mechanism. If your friend is unsure as to why she is sad, or empty, or crying, and feels hopeless, or out of control, then it may be necessary for her to pay closer attention to her mental wellbeing.

4/ Am I uncharacteristically irritable, or are those around me suggesting that I am more irritable than usual?

Let's face it, some of us just are quite irritable; I know that, for much of the time, I am. When I feel emotionally vigorous, though, then comments that would otherwise offend or aggravate me tend to bounce right off. On the other hand, when I am tense and irritable, everything seems to go wrong. People frequently offend me with their words and actions. I can open a cupboard, and something will fall out, crashing to the floor and smashing into a thousand pieces. I trip or bang into things. I put things down and lose them moments later. Our behaviour is affected so negatively when we are tense or angry, and outside events seem sometimes in collusion to exacerbate our mood. But what comes first, the chicken or the egg? Do minor catastrophes jump on the band wagon of despair, or does a foul mood cause the frequent mishaps. I am apt to believe that our mood dictates many events that unfold around us; another solid reason for investing in the maintenance of our resilience.

5/ Am I lacking energy?

Again, this answer to this should bear in mind your natural state. It's the sudden changes that are the red flags for low mood or depression.

6/ Do I ever think about suicide or have other dark thoughts?

This can be a tricky one, as many people will find it very difficult to admit to such thought processes, and, if they do, they may feel that this terrible confession could trigger a dramatic reaction that they could well do without.

I have no problem with admitting that I frequently have such thoughts. I have an active imagination, though, and I frequently have all kinds of thoughts. I have never considered or attempted suicide, and here is the huge difference. I am sure that many people have from time to time entertained scenarios where they simply lay down, drift into eternal slumber, and are absolved of all of the problematic minutiae of life. In the event that the thought becomes compulsive, though, things become more serious. If such dark thoughts are revisited again and again, or if the thought becomes a consideration, a plan, or even an act, then of course this situation requires immediate professional intervention.

Genuine friendship is not always about laughter and frivolity. It takes a good friend to alert someone to these red flags of emotional vulnerability. My guess is that your friend is highly likely to welcome an opportunity to talk about her deepest feelings, and will be deeply grateful to you for having the courage to open up a frank conversation.

Either way, her realisation that all is not well can be the first stage of your friend's reclamation of her vibrant fun-loving personality. I needn't tell you that she will not be the only winner in this scenario. Her child will benefit from growing up in the bright light of her happiness and enthusiasm, and you, her dearest, most honest friend, can again stake a claim in your share of the good times.

Whenever I notice that my energy levels are low, that my thought processes are gloomy and my appetite for fun has all but dwindled away, I move from my depression check-list to my 'quick fix' check list. It seems too simple to be true, but even after I have made the decision to make the minor adjustments on my list, I immediately begin to feel better. I have a plan, and, like many people with autistic traits, a plan is sometimes all I need to begin to feel that I am back in the saddle. A few days into the new routine, and I am generally back to my creative, enthusiastic self, looking ahead with hope and excitement, and fully able to plan for the future.

So here is my quick fix list – your friend's may differ slightly, but most people will gain advantage from making adjustments in these areas.

How is my diet?

I hereby admit a fondness for stodgy take-aways, large glasses of red wine, family sized bars of chocolate, and other nasties. When a quick fix becomes imperative, I swap the donuts and the pasties for ripe tomatoes, avocados, rainbow salads that are crisp and enticing, nuts, seeds and smoothies, and soon notice that the things that I crave change in accordance with my revised diet. My evening glass of wine becomes an evening cup of tea, and three days down the line, my outlook is already sunnier, and I am feeling energised and hopeful once again.

1. Am I getting enough fresh air and exercise?

Until quite recently I used to run every day, but the two slipped discs in my spine and the warning that the back specialist gave me afterwards put paid to that. Even though I am not able to exercise quite as vigorously now, mild exertion is not out of the question. I make time go out for two walks each day, taking the dog and the children with me. I choose somewhere beautiful, somewhere that will lift my spirits. I breathe deep of the fresh air, and challenge myself to notice the beauty around me. I listen to the sound of the birds, instead of just letting it wash over me. I look at the trees, at the delicate flowers, at the shapes that the clouds make in the sky. If I am lost for inspiration, I follow Lenny's expert gaze. My Wizard-boy is attuned to the magic of nature, and I need only look towards whatever has captured his attention to discover something breath-taking.

2.   How is my sleep?

With so much to do, and with children who don't always sleep well themselves, getting an early night can prove to be difficult. It's not impossible though. Because of the help that we get from respite services, in the event of an emotional dip, I can use this time to catch up on sleep. Something in me screams that this is a waste of a perfectly good, free night! But my renewed energy levels the next day tell a completely different story.

3.   Have I engaged in any creative activity?

People often think too elaborate when they think 'creativity.' A creative endeavour doesn't always have to include a well-stocked craft cupboard or an alarmingly masculine toolbox. I find the new adult colouring in books to be very therapeutic. I recommend them to all of my friends who are coping with stressful lives. Creativity to me often centres on cooking. Delicious food is such a practically sensible thing to create, there is always going to be a use for it, even among the very selective members of my family. I hole myself up in the kitchen, pour a nice glass of merlot, and set about making something that looks and tastes amazing. I also love to write; poems, short stories, and plays. There is something about creating that, to me, seems the opposite, the antidote to depression. Creation is Life, and depression seems to be withdrawal from life. So, if you, or your friend, tick too many worrying points on the check list to turn a blind eye to, plan something creative together.

I learned a very uplifting activity from a group of friends who help to run the wonderful 'A Day In My Shoes' course. The course is available to parents of disabled children in our area, and helps them to take a step away from their lives, to assess the balance, and, in short, to make sure that they are making time for the things that make life worth living. The ladies who deliver this course each make a 'Life Map,' a simple roll of paper on which they plot their journey so far. Photographs, their own words, cut-outs from magazines, concert tickets and other memorabilia illustrate their voyage. I found creating this straightforward, visual storyboard to be very helpful. I have even shown mine to a few of my friends, so that they are better able to understand where I am coming from. At a glance, it is easy to see that any troughs are generally followed by peaks, that any tough times provide us with valuable coping skills for what comes next.

4.   Have I treated myself to anything luxurious lately?

Depressed people can altogether forget the sheer pleasure of a glossy new hairdo or a flattering new dress. It might not even occur to your friend to embark on a shopping trip, and if you drag her along it may take some persuading for her make the effort to try on new clothes. Give it a go, though, if she is at all willing. Although it may seem shallow, seeing the reflection of ourselves looking happy, well dressed, and hopeful can trigger a mirrored reaction in our real selves. It has happened to me on a number of occasions. I have glanced and seen someone I had almost forgotten existed. Someone fun and funny, someone who loves to dress nicely, entertain and engage with people. Remember her? She was great! I wouldn't mind having her back in my life, every now and again, to cheer me up.

5.   Am I spending time with the people who make me feel good about myself?

I hope that, for your friend, you are, or can become that person. If her sparkle has all but winked out, though, you may need some help to gently blow the embers of her soul and get that fire going again. Whoops, that sounded a bit sexual, but you know what I mean. Recruit a gang of her favourite people. Share some of yours with her, if necessary. Plan something, a fun night in, a show, a wonderful meal. Surround her with the flame of enthusiasm and see if it catches on. I know that, for myself, being around enthusiastic people is an absolute tonic. I am soon sucked in. When I feel waves of genuine excitement radiating from my friends, it is difficult for me to remain pessimistic for long.

6.   Is there something on my mind? Have I the courage, or the opportunity speak about it?

It's crazy but true, some of the things that worry or bother us the most are the least likely topics up for discussion. To the worried or depressed person, it is as though putting our worst fears into words and bringing them forth into the world might somehow manifest their reality. Airing our fears is always positive though, and can be a great way to access help or expert advice. Sitting on our fears actually makes things worse, the seed of doubt germinates within us, becoming something dark, hidden and monstrous. Be the one to ask frankly what's bothering your friend. Reassure her that nothing is unsayable, that you will listen with an open mind and heart to even her darkest, most ridiculous fears. Once she feels free to say the words out aloud, whatever she had been worrying about may become instantly lighter. That outcome that she had feared may seem ludicrously implausible.

This has happened to me many time. For the longest time I nursed a silent fear that the children would be removed from our care. Over time, the expertise needed to care for them has become more and more specialised. My worry was that professionals would consider it too big a job, and that they would intervene, suggest some type of institution or residential school arrangement. Richard's amazed, almost amused, reaction when I finally voiced this concern made my deepest fear seem instantly far-fetched. I went on to talk through the hidden fear with my friend who laughed heartily. 'Nobody in their right mind would take them off you!' she said, breezily. When I asked what made her so sure, she said that if they were to take them away, then they would have to look after them. The lighthearted reassurance helped to chase away the dark thought that had been haunting me for so long.

Please do not feel offended by these basic suggestions. I know that true, dark depression is not nearly so easily fixed. I have shared with you my personal checklist for symptoms, and action list for remedies in the hope that, with your help and guidance, adopting this fairly rigorous approach to mental and emotional wellbeing will become a useful habit for your friend.

She has a worthy and challenging task ahead of her, and, as the old saying goes, If the ship is to stay afloat, then the captain must first look after himself.

Empathy and the Autist

Let us now address this rumour, this preconception that those on the autistic spectrum have no empathy. It's important to me to do my part in dispelling this myth, as I believe it to be damaging and dangerous.

To imagine that a person is robot-like, without feeling or the capacity for love, is to dehumanise our idea of the autist. This supposition places those on the spectrum beneath, or at the very least, apart from the rest of society.

The ability to empathise, or show empathy, for sure, is one of the personality facets that can seem to be 'off kilter' when someone has autism. Apparent lack of empathy has been used as a 'red flag' for children, who later go on to be assessed.

My understanding (based on nothing more than my years of experience as a mum and friend of people on the spectrum) is that while one autist can appear to have no empathy, a complete lack of concern for another person's feelings or understanding of their perspective, there can be another with so much empathy that they are crippled by their experience of other people's pain. This is beautifully illustrated by my youngest and eldest children.

Lenny remains completely unmoved by the usual parental blackmail ('be a good boy for Mummy' – 'Mummy will be cross!') Picking apart this lack of concern for whether I am pleased with his behaviour or not, it soon becomes clear that the basic parenting tool that we use to encourage our children to behave in the desired way is the manipulation of empathy. If empathy seems to be absent, or inaccessible because of a lack of understanding, us parents are rendered tool-less, or at the very least, we find ourselves in a position where we must utilise alternative tools.

Over the years, Rosie has suffered greatly for her excessive empathy. She feels so deeply, so intensely that at times she has been unable to differentiate between other people's emotional pain and her own.

Only when it appears to be missing do we realise how very much our child-rearing methods rely on a child's natural yearning to please us. What if your child really doesn't care if you're cross or not? What if he walks right out of the naughty corner every time you place him there, seemingly deaf to your strict 'Super Nanny' tone? What if the old fashioned smack on the bottom delights him, to the point where he jumps up and down, excited by the physical sensation? I have heard the phrase 'All he needs is a firm hand' many a time with regard to my son. It used to infuriate me. How could anyone assume that I, who am the person on this planet most negatively affected by my children's sensory driven, chaos-inducing behaviour, would not somewhere along the line, have tried exerting a little discipline? Nowadays, I simply smile in response to this suggestion. I wonder, how firm a hand would it have to be, in order to glean the desired reaction? And would this level of firmness even be legal?

Of course, without the illuminating two decades of experience as an autism mum behind me, mine might well be one of those irritating voices urging other people to try the 'firm hand' approach.

Excessive empathy, I believe, can be a harder condition to live with than the apparent lack of. It was the cause of an inordinate amount of pain for Rosie as a younger child, and even today she becomes off-the-scale furious when she learns about social injustice. Although this is hurtful to her, and causes her much in the way of anguish, I'm beginning to realise that it is not wholly a bad thing. It is this outrage at discrimination and inequality that has spurred her on to work so hard towards her awareness raising campaign. She has had to overcome crushing social anxiety in order to deliver her speeches and seminars to wide audiences around the world. I often reflect that if she didn't have this overpowering hatred of injustice, or such deeply sensitive empathy, then she would never have been moved to forge changes in a generation's understanding of what it means to be different.

When she was a little girl, if ever I left her to watch TV while I cracked on with my chores, I would have one ear open for the piercing cry of anguish that would inevitably be heard over the noise of the washing machine and hoover. Social injustice, even then, was her main trigger. Bizarrely, children's cartoons are jam-packed with examples of this. If a character was blamed for something that he/she hadn't done, and his cries of innocence were disbelieved, then this unfairness would prompt Rosie's waves of howling distress. Boy, could she cry.

Her hollering would set off a back-up chorus of wails from her brother and sister, and my home would plunge into instant anarchy. It was as though she couldn't bear the pain of another person's sadness, even if that 'person' was only nothing but an animated character. She would cover up illustrations in books with her hand, if the character had a sad expression. Even a simple line drawing, two 'eye dots' and a turned down dash for a mouth could catapult her into despair. She found rock music threatening, graffiti terrifying. She seemed tuned into sadness and horror. Ironically she now plays in a rock band and writes short horror stories in her spare time – it's funny how things can turn around.

Interestingly, this extreme reaction to the witness of social injustice has been identified in a new checklist of the less obvious character traits of girls with high functioning autism.

Of course, my youngest and eldest children's examples of apparent lack of empathy and empathy overload are only the most extreme points on a continuum. Every point in between is occupied by one autist or another. An empathy spectrum within the autism spectrum, if you like.

This is true of so many other facets of personality or ability.

An autist's intellectual ability can range anywhere from the profoundly disabled mark to creative prodigy – the much talked about autistic savant. As many autism mums are only too aware, one child may be so sensitive to the flavours of food that he will choose only the blandest, most predictable of meals, while another may seek sensory gratification from very spicy or flavoursome foods. Someone can be extremely sensitive to sound, to the point where it is every day practice to wear ear defenders, and another person might crank the music speakers up to maximum volume for the sheer pleasure of the noise (Lenny loves to place his cheek against speakers, absorbing his beloved music through his skin via vibration as well through his ears). One autist may be so socially disinhibited that she needs advice on who is safe to embrace, on what subjects it is OK to talk about. She may need guidance when it comes to respecting other people's personal space, or keeping herself safe from those who might take advantage. Someone else may be totally introverted, hiding their face from others, refusing to speak or even make eye-contact.

A high tolerance to one stimulus can be coupled with an extremely low tolerance of another. To make it more complex still, someone can exhibit different reactions to the same stimulus at different times, typically becoming more sensitive when stressed.

These sliding scales of ability and tolerance are part of what makes autism such an elusive condition. It takes us back to the famous quote, 'You meet one person with autism, and you have met one person with autism.'

From the inexpert and patched together picture that I paint, you begin to understand why autism is so difficult a condition to pin down, and why even the experts can never truly be experts. The more people on spectrum that I meet and get to know, the clearer it becomes to me that each autist is different, unique. Just as each neurotypical person is unique. Your best efforts as a friend/aunty/grandma (buying and reading this book – attending workshops – learning all you can about the condition) will always be trumped by the simple (delightful, challenging, life-changing) practice of spending time with your fledgling autist, by being an active listener and observer. By placing yourself on level ground with him, holding back from the teaching, and being prepared to learn.

To return to the question of empathy, I firmly believe that to assume a lack of empathy because of an atypical reaction to someone else's pain is an assumption too far.

To illustrate, my son does not react typically to his own physical pain, but it would be dangerous and foolish to conclude that that pain doesn't exist.

I've seen him slip and scrape his shin bone on an evilly sharp concrete step. It was the kind of injury that makes the onlooker wince and the injured party howl like a trapped animal. You witness this accident, screw up your face, hold your breath and wait for the scream. I waited, but Lenny's scream never came. He looked puzzled for a few moments, shocked into inaction. He then bent over, peering closely at the pooling crimson gash on his leg with interest, as though examining an extremely beautiful, potentially dangerous insect. He slapped the bleeding wound, as though insulted by its oozing presence on his leg. After this he simply went about his business, oblivious to the dripping scarlet trail that he left behind. It never occurred to him to scream, to make a fuss. He didn't think to come and ask for help or sympathy. His reaction to the accident was unusual, but there was a reaction.

Lenny is rarely ill. There have been occasions where every other member of our family has fallen foul of some tummy bug or nasty virus and Lenny has apparently dodged the microscopic bullets. The viral journey can be measured as it makes its way around the inhabitants of a household ('Ah, you're past the vomiting phase, you may be wiped out for another twelve hours, but you should be fine in the morning.') Viruses usually seem to live the same predictable life within the body of each unlucky host. Not the case with my son, however. Shortly after it becomes apparent that the uninvited guest has arrived, it is promptly shown the door ('Not today, thank you!')

Feeling very queasy myself one day, I remember standing at the kitchen sink watching on as Lenny bounced vigorously on the trampoline. All at once, he vomited, an impressive gush of orange juice and assorted semi-digested slop. The sick splattered his Buzz Lightyear pyjamas, made the nylon mesh of the trampoline slick, but my boy kept on bouncing. In the same way that he is affected by viruses (an atypical way), I feel that he is affected by other people's pain. I sense the understanding there, deep within him, but this understanding doesn't affect his behaviour in the traditional way. I believe that Lenny feels everything that I do, it's just that his communication is so alien, so other, that many things get lost in translation.

I recall sobbing one time as news footage of a terrible disaster was shown on the breakfast news. Lenny sat very close to me, examining my face with interest. Suddenly he lunged forwards. I thought I was going to get a hug, but no. Instead he licked my tears. Again, this was an atypical reaction but touching nonetheless.

Rosie and I both get very disillusioned with the media's stereotypical depiction of the person with autism or Asperger's. Emotionally vacant, robotic geeks, dressed goofily for added comedy. Their inability to 'read' other people's motives and moods is the hilarious punch line to every sitcom joke (you know the show that I'm talking about). The typecast nerd stares blankly through jam jar bottom glasses, not in on the joke, deaf to the canned laughter echoing round the studio. Do we really want to add our voices to this derision?

I envisage an audience of the future shaking their heads in disbelief, just as we do now when they re-run old episodes of *Love Thy Neighbour* and *Bless This House*. We are dumbfounded by this recorded evidence of the misogyny and racism that our parents and grandparents seemed to accept as harmless banter. In an ideal world, my enlightened television viewers of the (not too distant) future will shake their heads and say 'How did they get away with that?'

Birth of the 'Dragon Mum'

The 'Dragon Mum' lives somewhere deep inside us all. Even the meekest, the mildest, and the most amiable of us are capable of incubating this ferocious beast. The inner dragon can be unleashed on society in a heart's breath, one second we are standing at the window, enjoying a pleasant sunset, happy in the knowledge that our perfect, innocent child is simultaneously enjoying this primeval spectacle, and the next, we are running, barefoot down the street, small, pointed stones threatening to pierce the toughly layered skin of our soles, chest heaving with fumes of noxious poison. Times like these, you begin to sympathise with Viking berserkers. Times like these, you know that you could annihilate a Viking berserker in battle in an instant, one swing of the axe and any number of those be-horned madmen would submit, rolling over to expose their soft bellies in tender compliance, surrendering to that beastly force; the autism mum.

We were standing at our bay window one evening, five-year-old Lenny and me, watching the colourful display as day turned to early evening. I was drinking coffee, him hopping from one foot to another, thrilled to the core with the natural beauty that was unfolding. Violet, silver edged clouds bowed with their great, groaning weight, threatening to spill their colourful burden onto the stage-lit world beneath them. The growling threat of thunder snarled and died, snarled and died. Secretly, I hoped for a spectacular electric storm, knowing that Lenny and I would make a very appreciative audience. The promised storm was taking its time to deliver, however, and I was partially distracted by an alternative drama on the telly. The magnetic pull of the television drew me further and further into the living room, leaving Lenny to his more wholesome, natural entertainment.

When next I glanced at Lenny, he was communicating with a trio of teenagers, who pulled 'spaz' faces at him through the window, drawing out their pink tongues, inverted-clawing of their hands, howling to themselves, self-congratulation being the order of the day; celebrating the absolute cut-throat wit of their time-honoured, bullying antics.

To drive the knife of hurt deeper into my belly, I saw that Lenny, unable to interpret their behaviour as anything but innocent, was thrilled. His pure heart anticipated nothing but potential friendship, and he waved and grinned innocently, forgetting the promise of the spectacular storm, intent on the forging of friendship with these despicable teenage delinquents.

I was out of the door like a shot. Barefoot and outraged, I ran down the gravelled pathway. Very shortly afterwards, I caught up with the fiends. I demanded to know what the heavens they thought they were doing (you are right, I did not say 'heavens') They could not answer. These teenage criminals shrank back and became frightened children. Before my very eyes, they regressed from cockiness, to uncertainty, to the 'we are going to be in so much trouble when our mum finds out' children that they really were. I wanted to kill then, but then as they became children once more, I felt weirdly protective. I called them very nasty names, of which I could tell you, but my publisher would blot out or ask me to pretend otherwise.

It is sad and shocking when an incident like this occurs. For me, one of the most frightening things is my own, unpredictable reaction. In times like these I have often felt that I don't know myself, that I am in danger of becoming out of control and doing something unthinkable, something that I may live to regret.

As time has gone on, though, I think that I am beginning to be able to control this dragon power. My children constantly teach me patience. I have learned to utilise that gap between assessing a situation and acting on it. I have learned to stretch out the gap for a few more seconds, in order to give myself time to make a sensible decision and to make sure that I act in a way that I won't lament in the future.

I am blessed to have had the expert help of some exceptional professionals over the years. Some of the teaching staff and therapists that have worked with my children have absolutely amazed me, and I am very thankful for their involvement, their professionalism and the advice that has enhanced all our lives.

Every so often, though, I will be forced to cooperate with a professional with whom I do not see eye-to-eye. Of course, this isn't news to you. We all have to deal with many different kinds of people, on a daily basis, and this is no bad thing. Remaining polite and cheerful throughout our exchanges with those who rub us up the wrong way is excellent training for life. If we can keep up this measured, amiable façade when negotiating our differences with certain individuals, it can only smooth the way towards a mutually satisfactory solution.

Nearly eighteen years into my journey as an autism mum, and I have now reached an agreeable state whereby I am able to put my occasional dislike of, or inability to get along with, certain individuals on a back burner. If the service that my children are receiving is adequate, then my personal taste in human beings is quite irrelevant.

I haven't always been this levelheaded, however.

I believe that the dragon's egg is there, inside all of us, slowly incubating, waiting for the right environmental triggers. The intense love that we feel for our vulnerable children, coupled with our anxiety for their well-being and the stability of their future, with a little soupcon of unprofessional or condescending behaviour from a person entrusted with their care; this chemical soup invariably causes the dormant egg to stir. Pile on the pressure of consistent professional cock-ups, attitudes that grate or infuriate, and before too long, the egg will crack. Behold, the dragon-mum is born!

I had heard the rumours, back in those early days when my children were tiny, and we as a family were still reeling from the triple detonation of their diagnoses. I heard time and time again that parents of children with special needs were universally disliked within the education system. They dominated meetings and saw their own children's needs as usurping those of the schoolyard masses. They invariably knew their rights and were aggressively determined to see any disagreement through to its most damaging conclusion.

Well, I genuinely could not see a time when I would be recruited into this militant army. If they even let me in, they would surely and efficiently soon expel poor, people-pleasing me.

I was feeble back then, empty and afraid. The world was an uncertain place, a place where any small kindness reduced me to tears. Unkind words had little outward effect, and I did not have the strength or the inclination to retaliate. I was so low that I felt deserving of the occasional criticism that was flung in my general direction. Hostility from professionals made me confused, ashamed. What had I done wrong? Surely, they were seeing something amiss in my parenting, or in the basic, wobbly nature of all that was 'me.' Clearly this judgement merited occasional cold sarcasm and criticism.

I know now that there are those among us who can sense insecurity like a dog smells fear. Instead of being moved to support or strengthen the self-doubter, then this breed of bullying tyrant tends to feel an instant superiority, elevated by the comparative depths to which the victim of circumstance has fallen. It's a deep shame, but the skill of recognising this haughty, arrogant bully (who can emerge in any guise; 'friend', doctor, teacher, nurse) is absolutely essential if we are to become effective, autonomous adults.

It was back in the very early days, when Daisy was little more than a puzzling newborn, that I first felt the dangerous stirrings of rage that were to become so familiar to me over time.

I felt no bond with her first paediatrician; I found him cold and completely objective. Some might say that these are good qualities in a doctor, but I much prefer someone with at least a perfunctory level of 'bedside manner.'

In the days before her diagnosis, I was desperate to take a peek into the future and get a glimpse of what life would be like *for* Daisy, what life would be like *with* Daisy. How much would she be able to do? How intensive would the care that I provided for her have to be? These questions would frequently keep me awake at night, so much so that I became ill and strung out through lack of sleep.

I decided to tackle the problem and made an appointment with one of our local GPs. I explained my dilemma, and the reason for my constant insomnia, and besides prescribing medication, (I wasn't keen, with my vulnerable new baby still existing solely on a diet of my own milk) he was at a loss as to how to help me. I asked if we could get any more detailed information about the assessment that was made of Daisy while we had been in hospital in order to throw at least a little light on the situation. The young doctor sighed heavily, tapped Daisy's details into his computer and then turned the bulky monitor to face me. I was able to read the initial observations that her paediatrician had made.

I felt light-headed as I read the heading of his report:

Funny Looking Child

This was the heartless phrase that the cold, insensitive paediatrician had used to describe my beautiful angel. Do you hear my roar? Even accounting for the fact that this happened fifteen years ago? Can you still hear the echoes of my rage? I demanded an explanation for the cruel use of this insulting phrase. The unfortunate doctor dealing with me held his hands up in the air, protesting his own innocence. Shaky with rage, I returned home, immediately channelling my vengeance into a letter to the hospital in which I requested that Daisy be transferred to the care of a different paediatrician. I explained that I could not even hope to have a healthy relationship with the author of that phrase. Two days after posting this letter, I had a call from the hospital saying they would assign Daisy a new specialist, one who they assured me worked very well with parents, and the offensive phrase would be removed from Daisy's notes.

Now I am under no illusion that my 'sacking' of this paediatrician caused even the slightest regret on his behalf, one 'funny looking child' less clamouring for his professional attention was probably a favourable outcome for him. I do like to think, though, that the way I utilised my wrath may have caused him to rethink the way that he refers to his patients, either on paper or in person.

I recall a school review when Daisy was on the brink of transitioning to the next level of her education. It was a well-attended meeting, with every manner of professional chipping in, contributing their own observations to her progress report. I felt under intense scrutiny, drowning under the sea of paperwork, struggling to absorb and decipher the landslide of terminology and abbreviations.

Daisy's class teacher, a young, freshly graduated woman who I had struggled to form any kind of connection with, took her turn centre stage and made the following announcement, directed towards me, but intended clearly intended for the wider audience.

'I'd just like to say that I am so glad that I have been able to get Daisy walking for you.'

Sometimes silence communicates the deepest meaning. I felt the egg inside me begin to crack. The dragon stirred. This young woman had 'got Daisy walking' – she spoke of her in the way that a mechanical engineer might speak of a piece of inanimate, long redundant machinery – 'Congratulate me, I got it going!'

As my face twitched with the involuntary convulsions of deeply rooted anger, and the room remained suspended in a gasp of silence, the young teacher and I regarded one another coolly. The clock ticked and papers shuffled. Noxious smoke was expelled through my nose and ears.

'I think Daisy can take at least a little of the credit for her achievements!' a disconnected voice offered, helpfully.

The rest of the meeting was a write-off, I couldn't absorb any further information as I felt the tide of indignation roll in. The matter was made worse when the teacher in question made some kind of perfunctory mistake with paperwork and then went on to justify the slip up by explaining that she was having a 'special' moment. Where could I take my anger? Something inside me went cold, and it was in this chilly desolate climate that the fire-breathing monster emerged.

Although I have laboured the point that certain words should not be pounced upon, innocent members of the general public should not be made an example of, and we, who constantly demand tolerance, should remember to afford that same level of lenience to other people that we meet, nothing makes me angrier than having to deal with a professional person who just does not get it. When professionals imagine that they can use any position of power to win personal battles or to get one over on service users who have previously caused them problems, then, fuelled by the fire of my inner dragon-mum, I am quite prepared to take these characters to the cleaners and hang them out to dry, but I must be on my guard, though. When things become personal, then a battle of wills between two parties can prove to be most destructive. It's a fine line between recognising shortcomings, making sure that wrongs are put right and becoming so drunk with your own power that you can no longer listen to reason.

You will see your friend change over the years. She must challenge things that are unacceptable to her. By degrees the world is changing all of the time, and this is partly due to individuals like her who are unable to allow incidences of incompetence, wickedness or downright stupidity go unchallenged.

My husband and my close friends have had to pull me back from time to time, to warn me that I am becoming overzealous in my pursuit of some small victory, that I am becoming entrenched in a battle that can realistically have no positive outcome. I'm often very grateful for these words of wisdom, these illuminating gifts of new perspective. As her wise friend, you can choose to support the dragon in battle, or to counsel her; to encourage her to breathe deeply and allow the noxious smoke of anger to dissipate in favour of diplomacy and peace.

A Tight Routine

I happily go along with the theory that with parenting (and in life in general) there are no mistakes. When we think proactively and creatively we can begin to appreciate that every time we 'go wrong' or make a mistake, this is a roundabout way of discovering a better way to go about our business.

A wise person taught me a valuable strategy for utilising that 'If I'd only done such and such' frustration. Looking back on a past event, if any regret absolutely jumps out at you, it is perfectly futile to spend any at all lamenting your error. Mistakes can only exist in the past, if you had the benefit of hindsight, it would have been nothing less than madness to plough on regardless. What is in the past must stay there; it can never be undone. Instead of regretting, my wise friend taught me to take this uneasy feeling, shake it up a little and use its energy as a tool for change. This quite easily takes us from a point of 'I wish I'd done that before' to a much more constructive 'This is what I need to change now'.

Looking back to when my children were younger, I should certainly have made the effort to provide them with a tighter routine. I recognise now that children thrive best when clear parental boundaries are in place. Yes, they will push against these invisible walls, but knowing that the rules are there makes a child feel secure, protected. And this is even truer of children on the spectrum. Remember their natural love of routine? Coupled with an innate mistrust of change? Then add the language and communication difficulties that can make the processing of new information problematic, and we begin to see how a tight, predictable routine can make all the difference to a young person with autism.

A lack of imagination can make the world a very scary place. For example, it takes a certain amount of mental flexibility to predict that after a day out at the seaside with Mum and Dad, the family car will be waiting to deliver you right back to your home, to the bedroom where you keep your beloved toys, back home to the TV set that knows to play your favourite shows, to a place where your beaker is regularly filled to the brim with your preferred drink. All these things are there, patiently waiting for the car that brings you, Mum and Dad right back, but for a child with no language and with limited 'theory of mind,' it takes a giant leap of the imagination to realise this.

When we use the word 'imagination' most people think of the ability to invent stories, to create works of craft or art, they think about the skills necessary for invention. The less celebrated, day-to-day imagination that it takes to predict what is likely to happen in any given situation is something that we tend to take for granted, until we enter the world of autism.

A sound routine does not only benefit the child. When we adhere to a predictable behaviour each day, mealtimes and bedtimes become something for the child to anticipate, the comfort of a familiar pattern soothes and reassures. When we engage in any familiar routine, be it mealtime, bedtime, dressing in the morning, or packing our things for a trip to the swimming baths, I see pure relief on my son's face. 'Ah, I know this!' Lenny seems to be saying, 'I know exactly what happens next! First, we collect our swimming things, then we jump in the car, then we get changed and then swimming, and after that, fish and chips!'

An outsider might misinterpret these smiles, this letting go of anxious, repetitive rituals, this willingness to give eye-contact and engage in interaction. Someone looking in might think, ah, this boy is very happy because he loves his fish and chip supper. But they would be quite wrong. Fish and chips are OK (so long as the waiter is warned against garnishing with lettuce, mushy peas, lemon wedges or other inedible atrocities), but what is really making my son happy is the simple fact that he knows what is expected of him, he can relax in the surety that he knows what's coming next.

I can't go on preaching the benefits of routine for another paragraph without coming clean. For the initial twelve years of my time as a parent, my family's routine was nothing but shocking.

Night times heralded the proverbial 'musical beds,' with all three of our children (often all at the same time) joining the marital bed. Richard and I (separately, or sometimes together) would sneak off as soon as everyone was settled, onto the sofa or into one of the children's beds, but it was never long before the pyjama clad assassins were alerted to the fact that we had absconded, and they would be back on our trail, hell bent on murdering the peace of our slumber.

I'm not quite sure how we arrived at this sorry state, but once a serious sleep deficit has been incurred, parents tend to find themselves on the treadmill of a vicious circle. It's a downwards spiral that they tread wearily, exhausted, woolly headed and ratty from all of the previous nights of broken sleep. Mum and Dad will agree to almost anything if it means surrendering to the oblivion of unconsciousness for a couple of hours. Chocolate in bed? Sure, no problem (Minstrels are good as they don't tend to melt on bed sheets). Telly on in the small hours? Why not? The construction of large towers, using furniture as convenient building materials and the curtains as handy, fabric vines to abseil to and from the precarious summit of these masterpieces of engineering? Well, OK, but please be careful...

You get the picture. I hold my hands up, it was a shambles. A desperate situation that came about not through any lack of care or concern for my children's well-being. Far from it. I adored my children. I would have died for them. If I could go back now, though, and have a word on the ear of my younger, painfully exhausted self, I would say that dying for them is no good! Pull yourself together, dear, make a plan and stick to it. Let the children know that they are not in charge, that night time is essential for sleep and relaxation, and, as well as being vital for health, sleep and relaxation are both really nice.

Back then I didn't feel confident enough to build a routine for my children, and they suffered a little for this, but we suffered more. I felt that they were amazing. Rare gifts from an unmanifested otherworld sent from some mystical place to enrich my life and to teach me. In truth, I didn't really feel that I was good enough for them. My current parenting stance of respecting and learning from the children has its roots in this early, slightly unbalanced perspective. They were my lord and ladies, and I was their willing slave, ready to lay down my worthless life in their service.

So, to return to my wise friend's advice, hindsight is a wonderful thing, but the reality is that there is no going back. Around five years ago I found the space to stand back and take stock of our lifestyle. It certainly wasn't all bad. We were together, we had remained resilient through circumstances that could have cracked our precious family unit. We had many moments of fun and hilarity. Our sense of humour was the fuel that kept the odd little vehicle of our household moving forwards. One day, however, would run smoothly into the next with little time for recuperation. Moonlight was as familiar to us as sunup. My husband and I were both medicated and on the edge of breakdown, and although we had pledged our lives to one another, and the perpetuation of family life was as close as either of us came to a religious vow, our marriage wasn't in the best place. Something had to be done. I knew that I had made big mistakes in my parenting, but the only useful place for this understanding was as a tool to forge some big changes.

The thrill of empowerment that I felt when, only a week into our new strict regime, the children began to sleep through the night! Lenny started to ask to go to bed at around 8pm! ('Meg and Mog?' he would plead, this being the show that he chose, and still, at nearly fourteen, continues to choose to play on his TV, while settling down on the evening in his room).

How much easier it was to bathe, feed, dress and pack off to school three children who were well rested and eager for the adventures that their day might bring. What a contrast from those mornings of old, dressing a dazed Daisy in her sleep, wrapping up toast in silver foil to be eaten at mid-morning break, carrying Daisy and Lenny one by one to their school bus.

My new routine worked like a dream. As the kids returned from school, I would have a bag already packed, nappies (yes, I'm afraid toileting is still a big issue), wipes, drinks, my famous bag of 'motivational bribes'. In the summer time we would go off to a local park or beauty spot, before returning to a pre-prepared casserole or sizzling chicken. In the colder months we would swim, or spend an hour or so in the library or local museum. We could visit a friend or relative, if we could find a willing host. Then we could come home for dinner with Dad, a bubble bath and bed. Oh, the joy of being in control. I could do this! The delight in finding that the sleep-starved zombie that I had been had emerged from the cocoon, a fully functioning human being!

So please, watch for the signs in your friend. Be alert, be an active listener. Ask her how she is sleeping. I'm not sure if the younger, zombier me would have listened to a friend's advice about the importance of rest and recuperation, but it's got to be worth having a try.

To have the energy to plan changes we must be in a good place, mentally. If you feel that sleep is a problem for your autism mum and her family, it could be very useful to take the children off her hands for a couple of nights. School holidays might be a good time. Perhaps you and he could get together to plan a night time routine for the children? She must never feel usurped as the main caregiver, but a little support can be the leg-up that makes all the difference. Her child, or children, once spirited away to a new and exciting environment (this is your home, if you didn't recognise my optimistic description) may be more willing to try the new routine. After a couple of nights of real rest, your friend will be in a much better place to implement the changes in her own home. Of course, only the closest of relationships will allow for such close involvement, and it's a challenge that only the most committed of friends will take on. If you have such a friendship, if you share a bond of trust and you are willing to put your money where your mouth is, then your intervention could provide just the space that your friend needs to build a routine of safety and comfort that will enrich and stabilise her family life.

Getting Away

The creative process requires space, rather than intense thinking. Creativity, I believe, is an essential part of who we are as human beings, and being creatively healthy really is the cherry on the cake of life.

There really is nothing like a short break or a holiday to provide this oasis of space that we need to shake ourselves up a bit, to take a fresh view of our lives, to make new plans and revise are old ways of thinking.

It is no coincidence that many people make life changing decisions or come up with new ideas while they are away on holiday. The change of environment, the break from the monotony of routine, together with the relative freedom from our day to day tasks, this combination of circumstance has an almost magical effect on our clarity of mind. All of a sudden, we are able to look at our lives from a fresh vantage point, to see very clearly what we can do make positive changes. This shake up of our mental state, I believe, is the true value of taking a holiday.

That, and getting a really good tan, of course.

Your friend, your autism mum, may well be very much in need of this space, this fresh point of view from which to evaluate her life, a place to make plans and changes, a place to gather her wits and her strength, and some time away from all of the mundane duties that go hand in hand with parenthood. The irony is that, for the family coping with autism, holidays are often far more challenging than regular, day-to-day life. It can sometimes be a whole lot easier not to bother.

Luckily for me I have a husband who has always been very keen on family holidays, and back in the days when my creativity and self-esteem were low, he was the one who sourced, booked, paid for and packed for our holidays. He would round his disinterested family up, attempt to infect us with his own enthusiasm, navigating, driving and singing 'ten green bottles' on the way.

Our kids weren't great travellers back then. The mere sight of cases stacked at the door would set Lenny off. He became confused, frustrated, unable to express his fears, not having the imagination to realise that leaving our house and all of his favourite things was not final. That, eventually, there would be a return journey. He would express his aggravation through rituals, getting caught up on those invisible thresholds between rooms, stepping back and forth and back and forth repeatedly, biting the heel of his hand, breathing rapidly, refusing food or drink.

Daisy was often ill back then and had direct access to the children's ward of our city hospital. The staff on 'B Ward' were like our extended family, and they were very familiar with her needs. Part of my reluctance to travel too far afield was due to the fact that I was fearful of stepping away from the reassuring safety net of their care. I would feel numb and fearful on these outward journeys, and I am sure that my family must have been affected by the gloomy vibrations that I was broadcasting.

On arrival at our destination my first job would be to go through each room of the holiday cottage or apartment, checking for hidden dangers. Breakables would be stowed away in outbuildings, or somewhere high up that the children couldn't reach. I would do a once-over of the garden, checking for escape routes, or other forms of danger. While Richard cheerfully assembled a rope swing in the garden to entertain Lenny, I would be fitting electric sockets with guards and checking the window locks. My negativity and over-protectiveness towards the children made me tense and uncooperative. In short, I wasn't in the mood to holiday.

Here I have to thank my husband for his diligence. As the years went by, I learned to enjoy the breaks with my family, and we have had some amazing times. Caravans and cottages, the occasional hotel and a few experimental trips abroad. Over the years, we have steadily established the routine of holidays, and instead of causing fear and suspicion, the packed suitcases have now become a symbol of promised fun. The word 'holiday' may still not mean anything to Lenny, but he joins in excitedly as we pack up the car, fast as a wind-up toy, speedy with enthusiasm as one by one he hoists the cases into the boot, making a peculiar high pitched humming noise that can be roughly translated as 'I am going on my holidays and I am going to have FUN!'

It has to be said, though, that when it comes to supervising the children, during holidays we are on even higher alert than we are at home. At home, Lenny has a 'safe space' in his room, a completely secure, padded, zip-up enclosure around his bed from which it is impossible to escape. This arrangement affords us the security of a full night's sleep, knowing that he is completely safe and cannot leave the house, or even his room. Lenny is completely happy with this arrangement, loving the cosiness of small, compact spaces as he does. Unfortunately, though, the contraption is not portable, so throughout any time away from home, one of us must sleep with Lenny, one arm and one leg over him in case he should decide to abscond. As you can imagine, for the parent on night time Lenny-guarding duty, this situation does not lend itself to peaceful slumber.

We have enjoyed a couple of specialised 'autism holidays' in accommodation with wet rooms, giant on-site trampolines and private swimming facilities, but even these customised breaks do not provide what are (to us) the necessary extra security of lockable kitchens. Is there anyone out there who is able to invent a portable lock, which will do no permanent damage to the internal doors and cupboards of rented holiday properties? I assure you, there is a lock-shaped gap in the market, and this device would make holidaying a whole lot easier for a whole host of families.

As well as guarding Lenny throughout the night, an accessible kitchen means that holidays must be spent on high alert during all hours of the day. The dangers are of fire and flood, sprinkles and scattering, biscuit thievery and washing-up liquid splurges in the kitchen. Our best form of defence is attack, and we tend to keep the children military-style busy throughout the course of the holiday, packing in so many activities that the opportunities for mischief are few and far between. Up, breakfasted and out in the mornings, a full day at the beach with picnic lunch, tea in a restaurant on the way back, then a long, country walk before bed. In keeping the children busy, and wearing them out in this way, we also tend to wear ourselves out. But this is the price we pay to maintain the cleanliness and orderliness of the holiday accommodation, praying, as we go, that we are able to keep open the channel of hospitality for a return visit. The trail of devastation that our children leave in their wake has caused us to be crossed off the mailing list of quite a few holiday letting companies, and as the years go by, our options become more and more narrow.

With all of the extra considerations that we have to take into account, we have had a few memorable holiday disasters in the past, but we are determined not to let these put us off going away with the children. Sensitive ears make flying a no-no.

Around eight years ago, preparing for take-off on a short plane ride to Portugal, Lenny kicked off big-time. It had been almost impossible to tempt him up the vertical ladder to board the plane in the first plane. After fifteen minutes of increasingly desperate persuasion, Richard had resorted to brutality, and carried him, fireman's lift style onto the plane. Once safely within the confines of the vessel, Lenny became calm again, fascinated by the many seats, the compact aisle and view from the windows. He refused point blank to allow us to fasten his seatbelt, however, and I tried to explain to the steward, who was having none of it.

'If your son doesn't sit down, then you will have to leave the airplane,' the merciless air-host informed us.

Of course, this was the cause of a considerable amount of stress for us. Our family of five lives on one wage, and we do not have the spare funds to be completely blasé about a fortnight's holiday being cancelled on the whim of a seatbelt-fearing five-year-old. The struggle to fasten Lenny in caused something of a spectacle, and a group of young men on their way to a stag weekend (as their loutish behaviour later demonstrated) found the in-flight entertainment highly amusing. Needless to say, Dragon Lady lost her cool and ended up issuing a string of profanities that alienated us from the support of our fellow holidaymakers.

We did end up fastening Lenny's seatbelt, again by pure brute force, and so we were able to reach our holiday destination. The whole of the holiday was spent in fear of the return journey, however. Daisy became very sick with what turned out to be viral meningitis, and the first day's sunshine gave way to torrents of summer rain that were so unusually severe that they made the local news.

Another time holidaying in Devon we took the children out for a long walk in the beautiful countryside. The walk was far too long for Daisy's unsteady legs to carry her, so, even though she completed parts of the trek on her own volition, we brought along her wheelchair. The hills were steep and numerous, up and down and up and down we took turns to push her. The uphill pushes were actually the least traumatic, but the steep descents, holding back the combined weight of Daisy and her heavy chair, to avoid the wheels running away with her, put incredible pressure on the spine. We successfully completed the trek, but later that night, climbing into a hot bath to ease the pain of my aching limbs, there was a terrible flash of pain, like forked lighting striking my back.

I was in agony and completely stuck in my half-in and half-out of the bath position. Even the slightest of movement caused instant physical torment. Somehow, I managed to ease myself onto one of the children's beds, and eventually Rosie came upstairs to use the loo. I shouted for her to get Dad, who was in the garden with the children. Amazingly, considering the remote setting of our holiday cottage and the fact that up until that time we had been able to receive no phone signal, Richard managed to get a doctor out to me, who prescribed sedatives so strong that the rest of the holiday was a blur. Looking after our children away from the home really is a two-man job, so for the rest of the break, Richard had to become two men! I remember being in a pleasant narcotic fog when he brought the children back from the beach towards the end of the holiday. Still unable to get up from the bed, I listened dreamily as he told me that the sea had become very choppy. Lenny had been slowly venturing too far out to sea as he excitedly splashed in the incoming tide. A large wave had scooped him up and swept him out ten feet or so. Richard had had to leave Daisy to her own devices for the ten minutes it took to rescue him from the strong clutches of the tide.

The drugs caused me to accept his account of the day's adventures with uncharacteristic serenity.

'Well, it's good that you were able to save him,' I said, resignedly.

I'm not quite sure how I survived the six hour return journey in the car, but I am sure that the strong painkillers helped. The episode was the start of a seven-year journey with intense flare-ups of back pain, which still recur to this day.

And still we persevere! My attitude towards holidays has turned around vastly over the past few years, as my overall attitude has received a vital shake-up. I love to plan holidays! I love the whole process, looking at properties online, researching the locality for things to do. Even the packing and the journey fill me with excitement. It helps that the children have also made the U-turn. Now, after years and years of similar journeys, they know the score. Once they have read the signs, pile of suitcases, jam-packed car, Lenny in the backseat (he usually likes to travel in the front, but his love of the same song being played repeatedly throughout any journey relegates him to the back when we are on a journey longer than half an hour) they know that they are in for at least a week of all their favourite activities, beaches, swimming, country walks and lots of lovely meals out.

So I am very glad that I stuck with the whole holiday thing and learned to love what I had previously cowered from. Another valuable lesson for me, and one which I wish that I could have learned much earlier on in my journey as an autism mum.

Which leads me neatly to the question, how can you best help your autism mum to embrace and enjoy her family holiday time?

Firstly, (and this is a biggy), are you close enough to her and her family to share their holiday adventure? An extra pair of eyes and an extra pair of hands are worth their weight in gold. Because our holidays are far from relaxing experiences, I don't have anyone who is willing to do this. I hope, though, that your friend's family holiday is less stressful, and that you are able to reduce this stress even further, by becoming an extra pair of hands, and extra fun person to entertain her little one for a few hours while she reads a book, or someone to babysit while she and her husband share an evening meal together.

Planning really is the way to go. For the reluctant traveller, we must find a way to reassure that the holiday is a two-way journey and that a return to home is guaranteed. Picture maps can do this job quite well if the child is non-verbal.

Journey planning can be very enticing for some children with autism, planning routes and looking at maps can be almost as motivating as holiday sandwiched between the outward and homeward bound trips. A visual timetable will support his understanding of the timescale of the trip. I have learned now to never keep anything from my children. The theory that springing a surprise on them to avoid a meltdown may work once, but eventually all sneaky behaviour breeds mistrust. Even if I think that our plans are going to upset the children, I let them know what is going to happen. To plan a holiday with her child's involvement is a good thing. If he has the understanding, researching things to do in the area together will give her little autist some sense of control over the trip, as will being involved in packing his own suitcase and carefully selecting which of his possessions are vital for his happiness and contentment over the coming week or so.

If and when I am lucky enough to take a child-free break, then I expect to have a relaxing few days. When we go as a family, however, I am fully resigned to the fact that, though our holiday will undoubtedly involve lots of fun and laughter, I am very unlikely to get even a moment to myself. Accepting this is the key for me, unrealistic expectations are a direct route to feeling grumpy with my lot. Once I am fully reconciled to spending seven days without any child-free time, if the odd hour of calm should present itself, then I am pleasantly surprised.

Looking Ahead

I vividly recall a conversation that I had with a lady from our village when Daisy was tiny, newly diagnosed and curled up sleeping in the back carriage of the first in a series of double buggies that we would invest in over the years.

'She'll always be a baby,' the kindly neighbour told me.

At the time I drew a lot of comfort from this prediction. I imagined the years spanning ahead of us, filled with tender moments, feeding, dressing, singing nursery rhymes and enjoying perambulated strolls through flower gardens. When we are full with the gentle ache of new motherhood, it is very difficult to imagine a time when this feeling will not be with us.

As documented, Daisy wasn't expected to be able to do many of the things that she does today. With her very soft muscle tone, her tiny inverted feet and her complete lack of desire to do anything except curl up on my lap, the possibility of her walking seemed like an unimaginable dream. It seemed unlikely that she would ever even crawl.

At around three and a half years, though, she did learn to crawl. I was out on the momentous occasion, enjoying a rare evening meal with my sisters. At the time Daisy was very motivated by food and had recently developed a liking for raisins. With me safely out of the picture, Richard lay a clean, white sheet down on our living room carpet and placed Daisy in the centre of it, with the tempting, juicy raisins just out of her reach. This was the kind of push that I never would have agreed to back then, believing that my incapable angel should simply be loved and pampered, never teased or taunted in this way. With hindsight, it is very clear to me that this over-protective stance did Daisy no good at all. The following day I was treated to a display of Daisy's new skill. I was amazed and delighted.

Her newfound mobility brought its own problems. Daisy has always explored with her mouth, and we found that we had to become ultra-careful about what we left hanging around. Among items found completely undigested amid the unmentionable contents of her nappy have been a tiny green house from the Monopoly set, numerous decorative glass beads and, most alarmingly, the stretched, blue blubber of a burst balloon. She once ate a snail in the garden. Uncooked. *Sans* garlic butter.

But progress is progress, and we simply had to up our game. We began to notice that, as she moved around more freely, exploring her environment, and autonomously exercising her body for the first time ever, she gradually became less susceptible to the recurring respiratory infections that had plagued her since her earliest days.

At five years old, Daisy took her first steps. It happened on a summer evening as we were enjoying an alfresco tea in the garden of a local pub. She had been sitting on a picnic rug, playing with some toys that we had brought along, when all of a sudden she pulled herself to her feet, using the table leg for balance and, very slowly, very carefully, walked. Rich and I were both dumbfounded with the shock, too gobsmacked to think of reaching for our phone or camera, but Rosie, practical as ever, counted her steps. There were seventeen in all!

Her health continued to improve as she spent more time standing and walking. When she had been little and stationary for the whole of the time that she wasn't being forced to do her physiotherapy exercises, I had never connected her recurring illnesses with the fact that she was immobile for much of the day. The more she carefully, steadily moved her little body around, the stronger her muscle tone became. Our hospital visits became fewer and further between. Our little princess was growing up, after all.

Children with learning disabilities are not perpetual babies. Even when I refer to Daisy's very early developmental age, I in no way consider that she is a baby. This method of pinning down a developmental age is actually an outmoded practice, and does not take into account the years of experience that a person may have had while loitering at any specific 'age' marker. Evaluating the skills that the average four-year-old has acquired, it is important to remember that he has been practicing and perfecting these skills for a mere forty-eight months. Even when a learning disability means that he is not able to move forward from this expertly evaluated stage, he will eventually knock up decades worth of practice. Whatever their intellectual limitations, children still gain in experience, they still reach sexual maturity, they still desire and deserve the highest level of independence that is possible.

I used to consider that it was a mother's job to provide the most perfect childhood imaginable for her offspring. I no longer think that way. Our job is simply to do our best; different circumstances and different cultural and personality settings mean that 'best' for one mum will not be the same as 'best' for another. Our remit is to prepare our children for the big wide world, and to bear in mind that, if the natural order of things plays out, we will not always be here for them.

From a very young age both Daisy and Lenny have been able to experience short periods of time away from home. During these respite stays, life is not on hold for them. While they are away from us, they continue to engage in all of the activities that they would otherwise be doing at home. They bathe and dress in the mornings, they choose and help to prepare and pack their meals, they board the school bus, have a full day at school and then return to their 'home from home' and their extended families. As well as giving us a much needed break, this experience teaches them that 'life' does not only exist within our home.

At almost eighteen years old, Rosie is now preparing for her independent life. She has secured her place at university, where she will study Creative Writing and English Literature. I must admit to some misgivings. Going back six months or so, I engaged in a relentless campaign to persuade her to have a year out. My argument was that she would be able to take advantage of the speaking opportunities that keep flooding in, since the success of her 'TED' speech two years ago. 'You will be able to put lots of money away,' I enthused. 'We can spend time together, without the pressures of studying, we can shop, go out to lunch, watch movies in the daytime.' My plan for her immediate future was perfect, other than the fact that I had not really considered that she might be ready to move on. To her credit, she told me – in no uncertain terms. The lady was not for turning; all the afternoon movies and shopping trips in the world would not divert her from the path of literary success that she had mapped out. Even though this shocked me at first, I now reconcile that if I, her mum, closest friend and ally, am not able to sway her from her chosen path, then nobody is. I actually take great comfort from that.

When it comes to the children and helping them to prepare for their futures, I must constantly review my own motives. I am reconciled to the fact that the children are not mine. Their lives are their own, and they must follow their dreams. Of course, because of their communication and learning disabilities, rooting out Daisy and Lenny's heartfelt ambitions for the future is a little more difficult, but, as I have learned and am reminded on a daily basis, difficult does not mean impossible.

Last year, because of the onset of his puberty and the added complications that this development brought about, it was decided that Lenny's respite allowance should be increased. Instead of receiving the standard three overnight stays per month, his entitlement was upped to two stays each week, with the visits always falling on a Sunday and Monday evenings. He also moved resources, to a much more 'autism friendly' setting, where routine is tighter, the same group of young people also staying over on the same nights each week. This way, Lenny is able to feel a reassuring sense of control; again, he is comforted by the fact that he absolutely knows what to expect. Even though I initially opposed the move (as his previous placement suited him well enough, and I didn't want to upset the applecart) I see now that this was the best possible option for my son.

Lenny will be fifteen on his next birthday, and I see a future where he gradually increases his time away from the family home, until he achieves full, supported, independence. We, of course, as his parents and legal guardians will be on hand to evaluate and regularly review the support and care that he receives. I very much hope that, along with his sisters, he will continue to be happy to return to the family home for regular visits, in the way that any typically developing young man who enjoys a healthy relationship with his parents might. Without the constant daily pressures of caring for two severely disabled children, Richard and I hope to remain healthy and alert well into our old age. We hope to continue to be able to provide our input into the organising of the children's care for the rest of our lives, but we keenly acknowledge that our children will outlive us and that at some point we will have to hand over the responsibilities.

Time sure speeds up when you have a family. The births of my children seem only months away when I take time to recall the details, the way that I felt, the way that I constantly wondered and worried what the future might hold for us. Being busy, busy, busy, the weeks soon turned to months and the months to years. Those birthdays kept on coming! No sooner had we cleared up the debris from one party than another cake was being purchased, an extra candle lit to mark the speedy passage of another four seasons.

Sometime over the next decade my household will shrink, will calm and will normalise. After gradually becoming used to the chaos, the constant noise, the fun and stress, the perpetual cleaning, laundering, sorting, reorganising and supervising, we will have to re-adjust to a state of comparative tranquillity, a late middle-aged, slower-paced existence. Are we ready for this? Not quite, is my honest answer.

When I was young, I believed that family was forever. I still hold onto that core belief – it's as near to a religious devotion that I get. Whatever the shape of the family, our bonds and our connections last forever. Childhood, though, can only ever be temporary. We must all grow up, and it is only right that we should all move on.

Beautiful People

I was first introduced to the fascinating dimension of autism at the grand old age of thirty-five, when my not quite three-year-old son Lenny was diagnosed. Firstly, I had to become acquainted with his differences; the different way that he acted, his different responses to the world around him, his unusual communication methods – complex, yet simple, sometimes direct, and other times comically 'round the houses.' I'm still getting to know my son if I am honest. He amazes me every day. He possesses a fascinating mix of brilliant skills and learning voids. These are chasms of emptiness that he will often not even look into, let alone attempt to fill.

A few years down the line from Lenny's diagnosis, I started to feel a basic acquaintance with autism. What was at first a frightening enigma began to take on the form of a familiar territory. When I learned that Rosie, my eldest child, also had the condition, the rug was well and truly pulled from underneath me. Much of what I thought applied to all people with autism, I found applied only to my son. Like her brother, Rosie had the classic 'spiky learning profile' excelling beyond comprehension where her interests settled but struggling painfully in other areas.

Like a starfish and an eel, Rosie and Lenny were completely different creatures. Two very different creatures, in the same sea. I swam with them, and I began to learn. I began to spot the subtle traits of autism in many other people. In the case of those I was meeting for the first time, who were new to me, the traits were blindingly obvious. When I noticed autistic behaviours or characteristics in people I had known for years, I experienced a series of 'lightbulb' moments. Another one of these lightbulb moments came when I discovered that autism could overlap with other conditions. Although Daisy had been diagnosed with the rare genetic condition, Kabuki Syndrome, just after her first birthday, I saw clearly that many of her behaviours were similar to her siblings. It came as something as an epiphany. A person can have Downs Syndrome and autism. A person can have autism and cerebral palsy. Developmental conditions were not mutually exclusive! Why this simple fact should have taken so long to become clear to me, I have not the slightest idea. It is very easy to understand that someone can have epilepsy and high blood pressure, hay fever and glaucoma. Why then, when it comes to learning or developmental conditions do we feel that we need to put someone in one neatly labelled box or another?

Autism is not only a condition of the mind but also of the sensory system. It is physical, as well as mental, and affects every aspect of a person's personality. The way that person thinks, feels, speaks, sees, hears, tastes and smells. A person's sense of balance. A person's spatial awareness. Their relationships to other people and to the world around them. It affects the way that they can communicate their feelings to other people and the depths and intensity of these very feelings.

If autism is a condition of the brain, or of the mind, then it hardly seems surprising at all that other conditions linked with brain damage, or inhibition of brain development (for example, Daisy's microcephaly) can go hand in hand with autism.

My three children are so vastly different from one another in their abilities, interests, and in the way that they look and act, that sometimes it seems incredible that they are all wrapped up in the same 'blanket' condition, or that they are all huddled together under the same multi-coloured rainbow. But then, at other times, I watch on as they sit cheerfully together, sifting through pebbles in unison, skipping around in circles, or dancing to the music of a much loved, often played song, and at these times they seem to be part of the same being.

I truly believe that things are changing for the better. Slowly, often painfully, we are learning the lesson that diversity is essential to the vibrancy and health of our societies. Throughout the history of mankind, any efforts to enforce homogeneity, whether in the arena of religious beliefs, family structure, or personal identity, have resulted in misery, social isolation, or horror. Only when we accept one another's differences without reservation, are we free to discover what commonalities we share. The healthiest communities are a pick and mix mish-mash of different cultures, ages, ethnicities, sexes and sexual orientations. Wherever there is separatism, there is pain. Before we begin to try to re-invent someone using the template of our own image, we must first break down the original.

To reshape someone in accordance with what we find to be to be acceptable is a misguided cruelty. If instead we are able to maintain a fluid understanding of the nature of humanity, even the nature of reality, then we will benefit as individuals and as an extended community.

I believe that every lifetime is a lesson. Some greater power thought long and hard about exactly what, and who, I would need in my life to best learn the lessons of autism. It's a broad subject; the student must complete many modules; acceptance, appreciation of diversity, deep communication, and an in-depth study of the senses that we take for granted, to name but a few. The student must also sign up for a whole lifetime of learning; each graduation day brings us straight back to the beginners' classroom. I constantly have to empty my mind of all that I think I am sure of in order to have room for the complexities of understanding that my teachers offer.

I am happy to take what I have learned so far out into the big wide world, or, closer to home, to lean over and offer the couple seated at the next table in the restaurant and offer a succinct and neatly packaged point of view that, if accepted and nurtured, could instigate a change in their way of thinking.

In the course of this teaching and learning exchange that it has been my great fortune to fall into, I have been blessed to meet many beautiful people. Young and old alike, people with autism who remind me at every junction that this tired old world, spinning through the dark desert of eternity, is not only populated by the greedy, the manipulative, the cunning and the selfish. Living among us are our gentle, mysterious brothers and sisters. Guileless, creative, imaginative and heartbreakingly honest. Peaceful and unassuming as deer in a forest. To learn from them, we must be still, we must put aside our cunning and our instinctive desire to play the game, to dominate and to win.

I thank you sincerely for reading my book, and for making it your business to help to make your autism mum's journey a little easier. Although in all probability I have never met her, I feel that she is my sister, and I genuinely value all that you do for her. To be everything to her, to take on board each suggestion of support that I have included in this guide, is perhaps too much to ask of even the closest of friends or the most loving of sisters. I very much hope that your autism mum has a handful of caring, loving people in her life who will share out the proposed duties among themselves. This way, your friend will never feel so overwhelmingly indebted to one particular person that the balance of her friendship is tipped over.

Being a mum of three children on the spectrum has stripped me bare. I have pulled away at layers and layers of misconceptions and falsities in order to be able to see the beautiful truth of what is before me. It has been an incredible lesson to learn, a lesson that I have applied to every other aspect of my life. My own children, their friends and the hundreds of other autists that I have been honoured to meet through my advocacy work, have all helped me in this process of shedding the many cumbersome layers of illusory concepts that I had blindly carried around for the three decades before my journey began.

Thank you again to my wonderful children, Rosie, Daisy and Lenny. I am richer, wiser and infinitely more patient because of you. I am able to see the real beauty in this world, and engage deeply and honestly with my fellow human beings. So; when it comes to this complex lesson 'Autism' there may be no graduation day, no point at which some black-caped professor finally hands my a fancily scrolled certificate, but my rewards for continued learning are manifold and priceless.

Thank you for pledging the gift of your friendship to someone who truly needs it right now. And thank you for joining me on this life-changing journey of discovery.